The Little Book of Behavioral Investing by

The Little Book of Big Dividends by Charles B. Carlson

The Little Book of Investing Do's and Don'ts by Ben Stein and Phil DeMuth

The Little Book of Bull Moves, Updated and Expanded by Peter D. Schiff

The Little Book of Commodity Investing by John Stephenson

THE LITTLE BOOK

of

COMMODITY INVESTING

JOHN STEPHENSON

WILEY

John Wiley & Sons Canada, Ltd.

Published by John Wiley & Sons Canada, Ltd.

The views expressed in this book are those of the author and do not necessarily reflect the views of First Asset Investment Management Inc. or any of its affiliates.

Wiley also publishes its books in a variety of electronic formats. Some content that appears in print may not be available in electronic books. For more information about Wiley products, visit our web site at www.wiley.com.

Library and Archives Canada Cataloguing in Publication

Stephenson, John, 1962-

　　　The little book of commodity investing / John Stephenson.

ISBN 978-0-470-67837-4

　　　　　1. Commodity futures. 2. Commodity exchanges. 3. Finance, Personal. I. Title.

HG6046.S676 2010　　　332.63'28　　　C2010-901888-5

Printed in the United States.

1 2 3 4 5 CW 14 13 12 11 10

Contents

Foreword   ix

Introduction   xv

Chapter One
Calling on Commodities: Why Commodity
     Investing Is a Savvy Bet   1

Chapter Two
Gettin' Goin': Companies or Commodities?   21

Chapter Three
Gusher: Investing in Oil   33

Chapter Four
Drilling for Dollars: Profiting from
     Natural Gas   55

Chapter Five
Going for Gold: Prospering with Gold
and Precious Metals   73

Chapter Six
Digging It: Making Metals and Mines
Work for You   99

Chapter Seven
Betting the Farm: Bingeing on Food Inflation   119

Chapter Eight
Ordering the Breakfast Special:
Finding Profits in Foodstuffs   141

Chapter Nine
Gaining in Grains: Investing in Grains   159

Chapter Ten
Bulk Up: Benefitting from Bulk Commodities   177

Chapter Eleven
Capitalizing on Commodities:
Why Commodities Are Happening   195

Foreword

PLANNING FOR THE END GAME. "May you live in interesting times" was supposedly an ancient Chinese curse. Historians really only write about the great events, usually disasters and wars, as there is not much of interest in peaceful, serene times. So, if the period you live in is interesting, it is probably not serene; volatility and the unknown become a part of the fabric of life.

Unfortunately, as far as investing is concerned, we live in very interesting times. As I write this foreword, we have just come through the worst financial crisis and most serious recession since the Great Depression. It appears that the economies are recovering in the United States and Asia, but there are rumblings that things might not be so good in the Eurozone. Many of its economies are in recessions, ranging from mild to severe, and the credibility of the sovereign debt of the Club Med countries is in doubt.

Indeed, just as we lurched from one bubble to another over the past decade, we are rapidly approaching the bursting of the next bubble—that of sovereign debt. While consumers and businesses are retrenching and the world of private debt is involved in the Great Deleveraging, governments around the world are running massive deficits as they try to stimulate their economies in the face of unemployment and slack demand. But there is a limit to the amount of money they can borrow and to the interest rates they will be able to pay, as the turmoil in Greece and the rest of the Mediterranean demonstrates. Even Japan will find there is a limit.

And we are rapidly approaching that limit. As investors, we must now contemplate The End Game. What will the investment climate be when the developed world is forced to deleverage? For some countries, it will be deflation. For others, it will be inflation. You can count on major currency fluctuations. Recessions will come more often and be more persistent. Unemployment will remain uncomfortably high. Interest rates? Expect them to be low until markets lose confidence in the ability of a government to repay its debt.

As Reinhart and Rogoff wrote: "Highly indebted governments, banks, or corporations can seem to be merrily rolling along for an extended period, when bang!—confidence collapses, lenders disappear, and a crisis hits."

Bang is the right word. It is the nature of human beings to assume that the current trend will work out, that things can't really be as bad as they seem. Compare how the bond markets looked only a year ago with how they looked just a few months before World War I. There was no sign of an impending war. Everyone thought that cooler heads would prevail. In a similar vein, just prior to the recent credit crisis, bond markets (and indeed all other markets) around the world were not signaling that the worst credit crisis in 70 years was about to emerge. And then overnight, so it seemed, the banking markets collapsed. *Bang, indeed.*

We can look back now and see where we made mistakes in the current crisis. We actually believed that this time was different, that we had better financial instruments, smarter regulators, and that we were so, well, modern. Times were different. We knew how to deal with leverage. Borrowing against your home was a good thing. Housing values would always go up, and so on.

Now, there are voices telling us that things are headed back to normal. Mainstream forecasts for GDP growth this year are quite robust, north of 4 percent for the year, based on evidence from past recoveries. However, the underlying fundamentals of a banking crisis are far different from those of a business-cycle recession. It typically takes years to work off excess leverage in a banking crisis, with unemployment often rising for four years running.

So, John, this is all very interesting, but what does it have to do with a book on commodities? Everything.

We have just gone through a lost decade for the stock markets in the United States and much of the developed world. What worked for so many years no longer does, yet many investors persist on putting the bulk of their assets in equities. The environment I have described above is one in which equities and index funds (which are the main way investors invest in equities) will struggle, offering nowhere near the touted long-term averages.

Indeed, if you went back to 1966 and invested in 20-year U.S. government bonds, your bond portfolio would have outperformed the stock market over the next 43 years through the end of 2009. Stocks for the long run, indeed.

What that says to me is that investors should look for ways to diversify their portfolios away from the current over-allocation to stocks. And one way to do that is through commodity investing. But simply buying a fund tied to some commodity aggregate index isn't the answer. And that's where this book by John Stephenson will be so useful.

To be a successful commodity investor takes knowledge—as much knowledge as (or even more than) it takes to be a successful stock investor. While a pound of aluminum, iron, or nickel is the same anywhere, the price can change based upon demand. The price of a bushel of corn reflects not only the demand for tortillas, but also the demand for ethanol. And everything is complicated by the world economy, because a growing Asia will need more energy and food, even as the developed world struggles to find that same growth. Which factors will have more influence?

Once you have made the decision about price direction, there are many ways to invest in commodities. Stephenson helps you work through the pitfalls and advantages of various funds and styles.

While I think the developed world is in for a Muddle-Through Economy, there are so many ways that individual investors can prosper—even in a sideways world. They need only to look beyond the traditional portfolio and explore the rest of the investment cornucopia. Volatility and nimbleness will bring you opportunity.

Arm yourself with the basic knowledge that is in this book, then dig deep and learn more. And as my friend Dennis Gartman says:

Good Luck and Good Trading!

John Mauldin

John Mauldin (Dallas, TX) is the President of Millennium Wave Investments. One of the world's most read investment analysts, his free weekly e-letter Thoughts from the Frontline *is read by more than a million people each week and is reprinted on numerous Web sites. Mauldin is also author of the bestselling books* Bull's Eye Investing *(978-0-471-65543-5) and* Just One Thing *(978-0-471-73873-2).*

Introduction

~

THE NEXT GREAT BULL MARKET HAS ARRIVED and it's not in real estate, bonds, or stocks, but in commodities. After the greatest financial collapse in more than a generation and a decade of decline for the S&P 500 stock index, commodities stand alone as the only *go-to* sector of the market. Best yet, commodities are an indirect play on the only region of the world that is experiencing explosive economic growth—Asia.

The heavily indebted West faces years of sluggish growth and a dismal outlook for job seekers. But for commodities the story is decidedly more upbeat, because commodities are the basic raw materials of urbanization and industrialization. Today, hundreds of millions of people are rising out of extreme poverty and, for the first time in recorded history, becoming global consumers, a good news story for commodities.

The New Normal

Consumers in the West had enjoyed a more than 20-year bonanza, one where real estate prices steadily climbed, interest rates fell, and employment prospects were good. But today, in the wake of the global financial crisis of 2008–2009, most consumers are deeply in debt and so too are their governments. Governments around the world have poured trillions of dollars into stabilizing their national economies, yet unemployment rates remain high in the West and economic growth is tepid. Western economies are in rehab after a 20-year run on a debt-fueled bender. Recovery is likely to be painful and slow as these economies shed the bad habits of racking up too much debt and saving too little.

Conversely, Asia's economy is rising and the prospects for commodities are rising along with it. China and India went into the global financial crisis of 2008–2009 in much better shape than the West. These emerging market economies had much lower levels of national debt, lots of foreign currency reserves, and consumer sectors that were in their infancy. At the beginning of 2010, China had a total debt to GDP ratio of 159 percent, while the United Kingdom's was an eye-popping 466 percent—a nearly threefold difference. Is it any wonder that Asia's growth remains unrestrained, while Western growth is sluggish?

The investment opportunities of the future will increasingly come from the fast-growing economies of Asia, not the stalwarts of the West. And that's good for commodities, the real stuff that makes economic expansion possible. The West has gorged on too much debt for too long. The repercussion of this bingeing will be years of slower than normal economic growth as the economies of the West are rebuilt. Between 2000 and 2009, U.S. stock market returns were negative and joblessness rose dramatically.

While economic growth in the West has begun, it's being driven by the government sector rather than by corporations or consumers. The unemployment rate remains stubbornly high and consumers are sitting on their wallets, terrified of getting walloped again. Can the traditional investment mix of stocks, bonds, and real estate really be expected to outperform in this low-growth environment?

In a low-growth environment, can the traditional investment mix of stocks, bonds, and real estate really be expected to outperform?

Nope. During the 1970s, commodities roared while stocks and bonds went nowhere. During that decade, America was strong, Europe was reemerging as an engine of global growth, and the economies of South Korea, Japan, and Taiwan were on the move. This time around, four-fifths of the world's population is emerging from an economic funk—creating hundreds of millions of new global consumers. Demand for commodities continues to surge. There are no substitutes for these critical feedstocks of industrialization and urbanization, and supply remains constrained. A powerful rallying cry will be heard around the world as investors clamor to be part of the next great bull market—not in stocks, bonds, or real estate, but rather, in commodities.

Dollar Downer

Helping to propel the bull market in commodities higher are an American dollar that's sagging under the weight of personal and government debt, which are in nosebleed territory, and investors' fear that the Federal Reserve (the Fed) will be forced to crank up the printing press to pay down the nation's debt.

Record low interest rates and a national balance sheet that looks positively sickly, with no immediate prospects for improvement, have conspired to drive the dollar lower. And that's been a boon for commodities—which are priced in U.S. dollars—as investors correctly reason that the value of *tangible* assets cannot be inflated away. The world may one day be awash in American dollars, but the amount of copper in circulation is finite.

To combat the recession and get consumers spending again, Uncle Sam has shot the locks off his wallet—spending money like a drunken sailor on shore leave. And with trillions of additional dollars hitting the nation's money supply, China, our largest creditor, is worried. Already they've publicly voiced their concerns over the direction the dollar is taking and its potential impact on their foreign currency reserves. If China ever decides that holding most of its reserves in rapidly declining U.S. dollars and receiving a paltry interest rate in return is a bad deal—look out. Were the Bank of China to shift 15 or 20 percent of its reserves into gold, or any other hard asset, instead—the dollar would immediately fall sharply lower.

Disco Days?

Disco and commodities share one thing in common: they both had their heyday in the 1970s. During that decade, while the stock market and the economy went nowhere, commodities were on fire—and so too was inflation. Millions of middle-class American baby boomers were entering the workforce, starting families, and buying houses, cars, and appliances—the stage was set for a long bull run in commodities. Germany and Japan were reindustrializing after the Second World War, and a growing global middle class was demanding houses, cars, and appliances—all commodity dependent. All of this helped make commodity investing the place to be from 1968 to 1982.

This demand for essential goods helped drive inflation higher. As basic raw materials, commodities are directly linked to the components of inflation, making them *ideal* inflation hedges. Inflation erodes the value of a bond and stock portfolio, but not a commodity portfolio. High levels of inflation are associated with booming economies and surging demand for commodities. Strong demand for commodities translates into higher prices for them, which more than offsets the effects of inflation. As a result, commodities provide purchasing power protection. That's important, because investors care about their real—or inflation-adjusted—purchasing power.

∽

Commodities, as basic raw materials, are directly linked to the components of inflation, making them *ideal* inflation hedges.

Today, many of our banks are a mess, and both the consumer and the American government face years of painful deleveraging as they try to work off the excesses of a debt-fueled bender. With government and consumers in debt up to their eyeballs, the prospect of a slow-growing economy looks increasingly likely. This economic restraint will slow investment, profits, and payments to investors in the form of dividends and interest. As America, and much of the West, enters a slow-growth era, buying a basket of S&P 500 stocks looks increasingly like a sucker's bet. Commodities, fueled by the fast-growing economies of Asia, should be *the* go-to sector over the next decade. Bell bottoms and disco may never stage a comeback, but we may be going back to an investment climate like the 1970s, when commodities soared and just about everything else tanked.

———————— ∽ ————————

While bell bottoms and disco may not be your thing, we may be going back to an investment climate like the 1970s, when commodities soared and just about everything else tanked.

Get Real

There are many things that I enjoy about being a portfolio manager, but I most enjoy the times when I get to leave my spreadsheets behind and head out of the office to see the oil fields, mines, shipping terminals, and natural gas plants that dot the landscape. The feeling is the same every time I venture beyond my computer screens: I always marvel at the size, scope, and technical complexity of these operations and at the critical, yet unheralded, role these assets provide in making the world work.

In spite of the crucial role commodity producers play in enabling the global economy, most of us know almost nothing about them; and what we do know is often jaundiced. In a world of glitzy new product launches and expensive marketing campaigns, the world of industry seems woefully out of date. Yet we have just lived through an era where Wall Street and its world-class marketers badly misled the investing public about the riches that lay ahead in cutting edge technology and high finance.

Commodities can soar when stocks and bonds are going nowhere and inflation is running amok. In a world of too much complexity and too few solutions, investors are looking for something simple, something tangible, where the accounting isn't flawed and the path forward is clear. As *real* things that you can hold and touch, things that you use everyday, commodities seem to be *the* solid store of value in these troubled times.

Best yet, armed with a knowledge of commodities you will be better able to understand markets, whole economies, and the world in which we live. More than an interesting niche area of investing, commodities provide us with an important window on the world of investing and understanding them transforms us into better investors; not just better commodity investors, but better stock, bond, real estate, currency, and emerging market investors.

Most investment books are long on theory but short on practical no-nonsense information and knowledge from which you can profit. This book is different. This book is about companies, about whole industries, and about a value chain that spans the globe and interconnects the markets of tomorrow with the markets of today.

This book explains the world around us—how it works, what makes markets rise and fall, and how *you* as investors can come out ahead of the pack.

The tried and true investment path led many investors to ruin in the 2008–2009 market collapse. What worked before is unlikely to work again. The world has changed and so too has investing. Commodities zig when stocks and bonds zag, and this often-overlooked but crucial part of the investing landscape is finally about to get its due.

This book is your blueprint for navigating the world of commodities—the world of tomorrow. It examines whole industries, how they fit together in the bigger puzzle, and what makes them tick. It explores the worlds of agriculture, mining, and energy, as well as the characters and countries behind the production and consumption of these critical raw materials. You'll learn the various ways investors can get commodity exposure and why these bets are likely to be savvy rather than foolhardy.

Commodities are already part of your daily routine—from the coffee that powers you through your morning to the gas that fuels your car. And from the farmer's field to the food on your table, the world of commodities is global and interlinked. Developments halfway round the world can have a big impact on the action in the trading pits of Chicago and on your portfolio. In short, commodities are a vital linchpin connecting markets and providing powerful signals about the direction of the world economy and the stock market.

And yet, they just don't figure as part of most investment portfolios. This book will change that. It will dispel the myths about commodities and make two bold claims—that commodities belong in *every* portfolio and that you ignore commodities at your own investment peril.

The goal of this book is simple—to sweep away the mystery surrounding commodities and expose them for what they are—the single best asset class for the next decade.

Chapter One

Calling on Commodities

~

*Why Commodity Investing Is a
Savvy Bet*

A MASSIVE BULL MARKET IN COMMODITIES is about to
wash up on our shores, powered not by the stagnating
West, but by a surging Asia. The big money of the next
decade won't be made in bonds or real estate, and certainly not in the so-called U.S. blue chip stocks—it will be
made in commodities. Savvy investors know that following global growth where it's going—as opposed to where
it's been—is *the* winning bet. And as economic influence

continues to shift toward the East, the smart money is investing in the basic raw materials that support economic growth—commodities.

A rapid reordering of the global economic pecking order is underway. In 1987, one-third of the world's economic output came from developing economies and two-thirds came from developed economies. By the end of 2009, their contributions were evenly split. By 2020, two-thirds of the world's economic activity will come from developing economies, while the so-called rich economies will be responsible for just one-third. The pace of economic change we are witnessing is both unparalleled and unprecedented.

―――――――――― ∿ ――――――――――

By 2020, two-thirds of the world's economic activity will be coming from developing economies, while the so-called rich economies will be responsible for just one-third.

―――――――――――――――――――――――

Commodities are *real* things that we rely on every day. From the time we get up to the time we go to bed, we are surrounded by commodities. The coffee we drink and the sugar we sweeten it with are commodities, so too are the steel that holds our cars together, the oil that makes them run, and the natural gas that heats our homes.

Nothing about commodities is bush-league; in 2009, the production value of seven of the most important commodities was north of $3.6 trillion. The value of the commodities traded on the world's futures exchanges dwarfs the dollar volume of transactions on U.S. stock exchanges. Commodities and the exchanges that set prices and marry up buyers and sellers of these crucial raw materials are so important to our way of life that the world as we know it just wouldn't be possible without them.

The value of commodities traded on the world's futures exchanges dwarfs the dollar volume of transactions on U.S. stock exchanges.

Plenty of experts will espouse the merits of stocks, the benefits of bonds, and the advantages of real estate. But when it comes to commodities, there isn't much of a fan club, despite compelling evidence that when stocks and bonds are going down, commodities are usually going up. When inflation is heading higher and bonds and stocks are heading lower, commodity prices will be on fire. Commodities have been proven to boost returns and chop risk in an investment portfolio, but even sophisticated investors give them short shrift. For most investors, commodities just don't figure.

Trading Places

Commodities trade on commodity exchanges, where they are bought and sold for *future* delivery. The first commodity futures trading can be traced back to 17th century Japan, where farmers sold rice to local merchants who stored it year-round. Not content to just sit on their inventory of rice, the merchants raised cash to pay for their costs by selling "rice tickets," which were receipts against the stored rice. Over time, the rice tickets became accepted as a form of currency and rules were established to manage their trade.

Almost 200 years later, in 1848, a group of Chicago businessmen formed the Chicago Board of Trade (CBOT), a member-owned organization that offered a centralized place for trading a wide range of goods. With its convenient location between Midwestern producers and the east coast market, Chicago was a natural hub for cash trading in commodities.

As time went on, buyers and sellers negotiated directly with one another to sell crops at an agreed upon price not only on that day, but also on a *future* date. These negotiated transactions, known as "forward contracts," are still a fixture in the world of commodities. As trading in forward contracts increased, the CBOT decided that most details could be standardized to streamline the delivery and trading of the contracts. Under this new system, price and delivery date would be the only variables.

The standardized contracts the CBOT ushered in were America's first futures contracts. All bids, offers, and transactions were published by the exchange, which increased the transparency and popularity of these marketplaces. With standardized contracts, it was easy to trade commodities. Investors who wanted to profit from a drought in the Midwest could easily use the exchange to buy futures contracts for wheat, and if their views changed, they could sell their contracts just as easily. Standardization was a boon to trading.

Commodity futures are standardized contracts that trade on commodity exchanges; price and quantity are the only variables.

Other futures exchanges quickly sprang up. The Chicago Butter and Egg Board, founded in 1898, later became known as the Chicago Mercantile Exchange. Kansas City, St. Louis, Memphis, and San Francisco all got into the act by forming their own commodity exchanges; yet today, Chicago still reigns supreme as the epicenter of U.S. futures trading. Globally, there are major commodity exchanges in more than 20 countries.

Yeah, But . . .

Commodities get a bad rap. In spite of their importance to the global economy, they are among the most misunderstood of all asset classes. Bonds, stocks, and real estate all have plenty of followers and universal agreement amongst experts regarding their importance within a well-diversified portfolio. But venture into the world of commodities, and you're into a fringe area of investing where understanding is limited and suspicions run deep.

In the 1983 movie *Trading Places*, Eddie Murphy and Dan Aykroyd team up to turn the tables on their former employers, Mortimer and Randolph Duke, by placing a winning bet on commodities. In a single trading session, Louis Winthorpe III (Aykroyd) and Billy Ray Valentine (Murphy) become fabulously wealthy while destroying the Dukes financially. To skeptics, reversals of fortune like that are all too common in the world of commodity investing, where volatility and complexity are the order of the day.

But peek behind the curtain, and most of the criticisms of commodities just don't hold water. While commodities are more volatile than bonds, their volatility is about the same as that of stocks. Commodities have no funky accounting, scandalous behavior by management, or incomprehensible off-balance-sheet items that can skewer your finances overnight. The problem with commodities—if there is one—is the amount of leverage investors can employ.

Leverage is a double-edged sword. It can boost your returns when prices are heading higher and tank your investments when prices are sinking. "Leverage," using other people's money, is quite common. For example, when you buy a house and take out a mortgage, you're using leverage. Both stocks and commodities can be bought on margin, but by law a stock buyer needs to pony up at least 50 percent of the purchase price. In commodity investing, margin requirements are skinnier—sometimes as little as 5 percent.

Suppose you decide to buy crude oil contracts when oil is trading at $50 per barrel because you think it's moving higher. You open a futures trading account, slap down the minimum margin of $5,000 per contract and—presto—you're instantly controlling $50,000 worth of crude oil ($50 per barrel times 1,000 barrels per futures contract). If oil moves from $50 per barrel to $55 per barrel, your position is worth $55,000 ($55 per barrel times 1,000 barrels) and you've doubled your money and are no doubt feeling pretty smart. But if oil goes from $50 to $45 per barrel, you've lost your whole investment. Still feeling so smart? I don't think so.

Wait a Minute

The Yale International Center for Finance, in their working paper *Facts and Fantasies About Commodity Futures*,* concluded that an unlevered basket of commodity futures gave as much bang for the buck as stocks. Not only did futures offer similar returns to stocks, but they tended to perform well when stocks and bonds were doing poorly. By adding futures to a well-diversified portfolio, the researchers found you could chop risk while boosting returns—a nifty trick. Because the value of commodities is tied to tangible assets, they performed well in inflationary periods, or times when prices were rising. Including commodities in your portfolio can not only help diversify it, but may also help you preserve wealth when inflation is gobbling away at the value of your stocks and bonds.

———————————— ∽ ————————————

Including commodities in your portfolio can not only help you diversify it, but also help preserve wealth when inflation is gobbling away at the value of your stocks and bonds.

————————————————————————————

* Gorton, Gary B, and K. Geert Rouwenhort, "Facts and Fantasies About Commodity Futures," Yale International Center for Finance, Yale ICF Working Paper No. 04-20, June 14, 2004.

In a separate study on commodity returns, Ibbotson Associates* found that adding commodities to an investment portfolio helped to reduce risk and increase diversification by generating superior returns when they were needed most. The researchers concluded that *all* portfolios could be improved by the addition of a healthy dollop of commodities.

Ricochet

Shell-shocked investors watched in horror as the commodity markets tumbled with the collapse of Lehman Brothers in September 2008. Executives at commodity-producing companies nearly went into cardiac arrest as their share prices cratered, forcing them to slash expenses just to keep their companies afloat—mines were closed, oil fields were capped, and steel mills slammed shut.

However, as the global economy picks itself up off the mat, the demand for commodities—the stuff that economic recoveries are made of—will soar. Commodity production is a time- and capital-intensive undertaking requiring extensive engineering, environmental, and permitting procedures before work can begin. Lead times for obtaining most major pieces of equipment are measured in years, not months. In addition, a severe shortage of

* Idzorek, Thomas M., "Strategic Asset Allocation and Commodities," Ibbotson Associates, March 27, 2006.

well-qualified people and investment capital means new sources of commodity supply will be a long time in coming. Sluggish supply and voracious demand have set the stage for our next bull market—one that won't be in North American real estate or blue chip stocks, but in commodities.

————————— ≈ —————————

Sluggish supply and voracious demand have set the stage for our next bull market—one that won't be in North American real estate or blue chip stocks, but in commodities.

A Bulging Middle

An exploding global middle class, fueled by global trade, is supplying the liquid hydrogen to the commodity rocket. Over the last 30 years, hundreds of millions of people have been lifted out of extreme poverty and transformed into global consumers. According to a recent World Bank report, between 1990 and 2002 some 1.2 billion people joined the ranks of the developing world's middle class. These people are not rich by Western standards, but are rich enough to leave a subsistence-level life behind and begin to spend. More remarkable, the report noted that four-fifths of this emerging middle class were from Asia and half were from China.

Others have predicted that the pace of this middle class expansion will accelerate, likely reaching its zenith around 2018. Goldman Sachs estimates that by 2030 a further two billion people could join the global middle class (defined as having a household income in the range of $6,000–$30,000). We may bemoan the decline of the American middle class, yet researchers at Goldman have found that the distribution of global income is becoming *more*, not *less*, equal, a trend that is likely to continue. The surge of the world's middle class is happening on an unprecedented scale. Affecting more than one-third of the world's population, the shift dwarfs the massive transformation of the global economy that occurred during the 19th century.

A mass migration is underway through much of Asia, as people leave the fields in search of better lives in the cities. With millions of new factory workers hitting the big cities, tremendous demand is being created for housing and other crucial infrastructure. This demand will underpin the boom in commodities as these new workers and their families begin to buy appliances, apartments, and cars. The last great bull market for commodities lasted from 1968 to 1982, when the Baby Boom generation was on a buying spree. But this time round, the scale of the economic transformation will eclipse anything we've seen before.

The key to understanding commodities is to understand China—a country that for 18 of the last 20 centuries has had the largest economy in the world. China is already the world's largest consumer of iron ore, copper, zinc, aluminum, nickel, and coking coal. It's also the second largest consumer of crude oil and the largest producer of steel—by a country mile. Not only is China growing at a furious clip, but so too are other emerging economies such as the Philippines, Vietnam, India, and Malaysia. Billions of people, all with aspirations like you and me, will demand the chance at a better life—and that's a good news story for commodities.

～

The key to understanding commodities is to understand China—a country that for 18 of the last 20 centuries has had the largest economy in the world.

A Decade of Decline

For investors in America's benchmark index, the S&P 500, the period from 2000 to 2009 ranks as the worst decade in nearly 200 years of American stock market history. Not even the 10 years encompassing the Great Depression was as dismal for U.S. investors as the one we have just witnessed. By the time 2009 drew to a close, the S&P 500 index finished the decade *24.1 percent below* where it had started—despite having two 50-percent-plus up moves. Investors would have been better off investing in almost *anything* other than the U.S. stock market. Stuffing their money under a mattress for safekeeping would have been a savvier move than investing in the S&P 500.

~

For investors in America's benchmark index, the S&P 500, the period from 2000 to 2009 ranks as the worst decade in nearly 200 years of American stock market history. Stuffing your money under a mattress for safekeeping would have been a savvier move than investing in the S&P 500.

The world witnessed a seismic shift in economic power during the first decade of the 21st century. The fastest growing economy in the Americas is no longer the United States, but rather, Brazil. Those who invested in the U.S. stock market at the height of America's power are poorer for the experience. First they suffered through the popping of the technology bubble and then the collapse of Wall Street. Global investors fared somewhat better but, because U.S. stocks account for almost one-third of world market capitalization, they too got caught in the downdraft. At the start of the 21st century, America's stock market capitalization was more than $15.1 trillion, but by the end of the decade it stood closer to $13.7 trillion. Over the same time period, the stock market capitalizations of both Brazil and China soared more than fivefold while India's stock market increased more than eightfold. And China, at the start of 2010, is set to overtake Japan as the world's second-largest economy.

Worse yet, America enters 2010 without a world-leading major industry. At the start of the past decade, America had two industries that were visible symbols of its economic preeminence: high tech and high finance. Both industries expanded rapidly, promising to enrich their employees, but instead they impoverished many. To promote their industries to investors, they relied on the notion that creativity was limitless and so too were profits. After all, American finance and technology appeared to be reshaping the world. America and its publicly listed companies benefited from the global perception that in all things that mattered most, America was simply the biggest and the best. But by the end of 2000, the technology boom that made so many people in California rich had quickly turned to rot. In the process, Silicon Valley became Death Valley, sinking the state's economic hopes and prospects.

After the tech wreck of 2000, Wall Street and the world of high finance stood alone as the engine for stock market growth. When the *Glass-Steagall Act*, which separated investment banking activities from commercial banking, was repealed, Wall Street's power and influence grew dramatically. Its dominance was reflected in its weight and overall importance in the S&P 500 stock index. By the end of 2007, the financial services sector accounted for 40 percent of all S&P 500 earnings—up sharply from its historical contribution of 15 percent.

Bond Blues

In the investment game, bonds are often characterized as the steady performers, great for cranking out solid investment returns but not as fleet of foot as sexy stocks. In spite of that reputation, over the last 25 years bond investors have had it good—they earned great returns and were exposed to very little risk. The golden era for bonds was the 25 years following the 1968–1982 commodity bull market.

The 1970s, on the other hand, were a great decade for commodities but not much else. Inflation was rampant, hitting 13.3 percent in August of 1979, and prompting a desperate President Jimmy Carter to appoint Paul Volcker to the post of chairman of the Federal Reserve. Only by ratcheting up the benchmark federal funds rate to a high of 20 percent in July 1981 was Volcker able to tame the inflation beast. In the ensuing decades interest rates were on a steady downward path, setting the stage for a massive bull market in bonds. When interest rates are falling, bond prices move higher, rewarding investors by giving them both capital gains and interest income. But can the party continue?

No. With interest rates on U.S. government bonds at multi-decade lows, there's nowhere for bond prices to go but down. Right now, central banks in the West are keeping interest rates artificially low in an attempt to breathe new life into their comatose economies, but eventually rates will have to rise to stave off inflation. And when interest rates rise, bonds fall.

～

With interest rates on U.S. government bonds at multi-decade lows, there's nowhere for bond prices to go but down.

The House Is A-Rockin'

In 2000, a wave of new, more aggressive lending practices had taken root in the U.S. real estate market, which, when coupled with loose lending standards and an easy-money culture, helped propel U.S. house prices into the stratosphere. For the average American worker, long-conditioned to expect ever-rising levels of consumption, the rapid rise in residential real estate prices offered a simple solution to the dilemma of stagnant wages—their homes could be used to plug the gap. As house prices were rocketing ever higher, homeowners threw caution to the wind and turned their homes into ATMs to fund their lifestyle—and no wonder, as real wage growth was stagnant from 2000 to 2007.

But economic disaster struck as real estate prices in the U.S. have tumbled hard—down more than 30 percent from their 2006 peak. Since the credit bubble of 2008–2009 burst, average house prices are down more than 50 percent in some U.S. cities. While the American housing market has started to stabilize, it still faces significant headwinds. A stagnant economy, weak job market, and a persistently high foreclosure rate are all major obstacles to overcome. Since housing accounts for 20 percent of the U.S. economy, an improved outlook will be a key pillar of any economic recovery.

What Am I Missing?

Most of the West faces years of slow growth and sluggish economic prospects in the wake of the greatest market meltdown in a generation. The last decade has been unkind to most investors. Stocks have tumbled badly, the bond rally has stalled, and real estate has turned out to be a sucker's bet.

But there is an alternative to investing as you always have; you can open your mind to the world of commodities, to a world without a legion of followers but with plenty of upside. Driven by surging Asian markets, sluggish supply, a sagging U.S. dollar, and few, if any, investment alternatives, the next great commodity bull market is now upon us. What are you waiting for?

Hot Commodities

- Commodities are part of our everyday lives and crucial to modern existence.
- Commodity futures are standardized contracts that trade on commodity exchanges. Price and quantity are the only variables.
- When stocks and bonds are going down and inflation is heading higher, commodity prices move up.
- There are legions of followers of stocks, bonds, and real estate, but there isn't much of a fan club for commodities.
- China is the key to understanding commodity demand.

(continued)

- For investors in the S&P 500, 2000 to 2009 ranks as the worst decade in nearly 200 years of American stock market history.

- With interest rates on U.S. government bonds at multi-decade lows, there's nowhere for bond prices to go but down.

- Commodity returns are similar to those of equities, but commodity returns are not well correlated to those of stocks or bonds, making an ideal addition to most portfolios.

- If not commodities, then what?

Chapter Two

Gettin' Goin'

~

Companies or Commodities?

THE GLOBAL ECONOMIC ORDER is rapidly changing—creating tremendous opportunities for commodity investors. Demand for commodities continues to grow despite the fact that much of the world is still licking its wounds from the global economic collapse of 2008–2009. Western governments have tried to paper over the problem of sluggish consumer demand by implementing stimulus programs intended to jump-start infrastructure spending, for example, the Cash for Clunkers rebate scheme aimed at the beleaguered American car industry. But despite these efforts, the collective credit cards of the U.S. and much of Europe remain completely maxed out.

The wheezing Western recovery aside, demand for commodities remains strong. Commodities are a big deal, much bigger than most people realize. Primary commodities, such as iron ore and copper, account for 25 percent of global trade. Supply has been sidelined during the global economic collapse, creating a near perfect storm for investors—a situation that is likely to last for many more years. As the basic feedstock for industrial and urban growth, commodities can be red hot even when stocks and bonds are ice cold. And with their direct link to the drivers of inflation, commodity investments are a heaven-sent hedge against rising prices.

～

Commodities are a big deal, much bigger than most people realize. Primary commodities, such as iron ore and copper, account for 25 percent of global trade.

Despite these benefits, commodities tend to be grossly underrepresented in most investment portfolios. To be a total investor is to know *something* about commodities—especially with a commodity bull market washing up on our shores. Yet commodities are a mystery to many investors: most haven't a clue how to begin.

Dumb Luck

One way to get into commodities is to luck out. You could find oil on your property as happened in the 1960s television show *The Beverly Hillbillies*, or you could stumble upon a major gold discovery. You might even inherit the family farm. In any of these situations, you'd be in the commodity business, but if you haven't yet struck oil on your swampland, chances are you won't.

Even if you do get lucky, you'll need plenty of help developing your find before you can pull up stakes and move to Beverly Hills. However, while it may look simple on TV, capitalizing on a producing commodity business is anything but easy. It is a highly sophisticated and complex undertaking requiring millions of dollars and decades of experience—not to mention good luck and excellent judgment. Owning a farm, mine, or oil field just isn't a practical way to add commodities to your investment lineup.

Go Along to Get Along

Investors love index funds and exchange traded funds (ETFs) because they mimic the price movements of their underlying indices and give investors an inexpensive and transparent way to get direct commodity exposure. There are several major indices and plenty of exchange traded funds to choose from.

The granddaddy of all commodity indices is the Reuters/Jefferies CRB Index, which dates back to 1957. The index has gone through 10 revisions over the years to help keep it both relevant and reflective of the underlying economic demand for the various commodities it represents. Most recently, in 1995, natural gas was added to the index while lumber, pork bellies, unleaded gasoline, soybean oil, and soybean meal were dropped.

In 1992, investment bank Goldman Sachs created a commodity index known today as the S&P GSCI. Another big player in the commodity index game is UBS, which has two widely followed indices: the Dow Jones-UBS Commodity Index and the UBS Bloomberg Constant Maturity Commodity Index (UBS Bloomberg CMCI), created in 1997. Jim Rogers, the Wall Street investment legend, created his own index in 1998, called the Rogers International Commodity Index (RICI).

A problem for all commodity indices is how to weight their various components to provide a *true* reflection of their overall economic importance. Most stock indices are constructed and weighted according to the market capitalization of their components. In commodities, however, the concept of market capitalization (shares outstanding multiplied by stock price) just doesn't apply. Commodities are held in a variety of forms, including over-the-counter investments, offsetting futures positions, and physical producer stockpiles—the combination of which makes complete accounting impossible and the calculation of commodity market capitalization an elusive target.

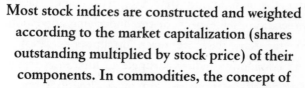

Most stock indices are constructed and weighted according to the market capitalization (shares outstanding multiplied by stock price) of their components. In commodities, the concept of market capitalization just doesn't apply.

Without the availability of market capitalization figures, commodity index creators have been left to their own devices, constructing and weighting the various components as they see fit. The result is a wide range of methodologies that can dramatically skew the weights of the index and its relevance as a barometer for gauging activity levels in commodities. Some base their weights on an assessment of the economic importance of each commodity, while others base them on a quantity of production basis. Subjectivity often plays a major role in this process, oil being a case in point. As the most economically important and actively traded commodity, oil's importance to the global economy cannot be overstated. In November 2009, the target weights for energy in the S&P GSCI were a whopping 67.83 percent, yet the Reuters/Jefferies CRB Index set its energy target weight at just 18 percent—a difference of nearly 50 percent.

Investors buy index funds and index-linked ETFs under the assumption that they will mimic the price appreciation they expect for the underlying commodities. Unfortunately, they are often disappointed. Not only do all commodity indices struggle to find an appropriate weighting of components, but most also do a poor job of measuring the here-and-now price movements of commodities. An investor who sees that oil prices are up $2 per barrel may justifiably assume that his or her commodity index fund is flying high; and if that investor is lucky, it will be. What all commodity index funds do is buy a basket of futures contracts, usually near-month contracts, which *should* closely track the price in the here and now (also known as the "spot price") movement of the various commodities. Unfortunately, they often don't. During the first 11 months of 2009, for instance, the price of crude oil surged some 73 percent, yet the S&P GSCI, with its heavy target weighting to oil, was a laggard—increasing just 46.88 percent.

**Commodity index funds should closely
track the spot price movement of the various
commodities—but unfortunately they often don't.**

Ready to Rock n' Roll?

You can make a lot of money in futures trading if you
know what you're doing. And if you don't—well, let's
just say you can lose your shirt in a hurry. Commodity
futures are just that: contracts for the *future* delivery of a
given commodity. While commodity futures prices often
resemble what's happening in the here and now, or the
"spot market," this isn't always the case. Complicating
matters further is the fact that most futures contracts
trade monthly and need to be rolled forward—unless you
want to take physical delivery of the commodity you just
bought. And discovering you're the proud owner of a
thousand barrels of No. 2 heating oil, currently waiting
for you at New York Harbor, can sure throw a wrench in
your weekend plans.

Depending on investors' expectations of commodity
prices, the futures curve can either be upward sloping (contango) or downward sloping (backwardation).
The futures curve is nothing more than a compilation

of individual futures contracts, so if investors expect oil prices to be going higher over time, then you should expect an upward sloping (contango) futures curve. If, many months into the future, the price of a commodity is significantly higher than it is today (contango), it may pay to hoard the physical commodity in the hope that you can sell it later for a profit. Oil traders and companies did just that during the 1970s when they hired tankers to store crude oil for months until they could sell it at a profit.

In commodity investing, the devil really is in the details, and the shape of the commodity curve is no exception. We've always heard that successful investing is all about buying low and selling high, but if you're buying futures contracts when the commodity curve is in contango, you're doing just the opposite. During the 1980s and 1990s, the futures curves for most commodities were downward sloping (in backwardation), yet commodity funds were posting excellent results since they were able to buy low and sell high.

~

During the 1980s and 1990s, the futures curves for most commodities were downward sloping, yet commodity funds were posting excellent results since they were able to buy low and sell high.

Figure 2.1 Buying Low and Selling High—It's the Shape of the Curve that Counts

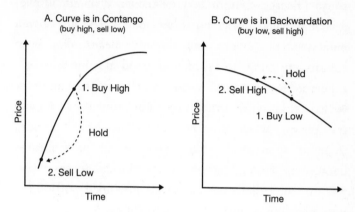

Managing the Future

Between 2002 and early 2008, commodities were back in vogue after a 20-year hiatus, and commodity trading advisors (CTAs) were suddenly in demand, moving their products faster than free ice cream on the Fourth of July. The idea behind managed commodity futures is simple. A commodity trading advisor manages a pool of investments, taking care of the pesky details like contract rolling, and giving you exposure to a wide range of products. Rather than studying the supply and demand variables for the soybean market into the wee hours of the morning, you hire an expert to make decisions for you.

Of course, managing futures contracts doesn't come cheap. There are tremendous benefits to obtaining professional management, but while some CTAs are proven moneymakers, many aren't—which means that your returns are going to be only as good as your advisor's expertise. Regardless of whom you choose, it's important to know that you're giving up both investment control and transparency when you use a CTA. If your CTA decides to move aggressively into frozen orange juice futures because he's spending winters in Florida, for example, you may find that your once well-diversified portfolio is now juiced-up on just a few commodities.

Company Man

So what's a commodity investor to do? Commodity indices and ETFs are easy to buy, but as I've explained, most have serious issues with weighting and tracking. If getting direct exposure to commodities by snapping up farmland in Ohio or panning for gold in Nevada seems like too much work, you should consider buying the stocks of commodity-producing companies. A key benefit of owning these is the leverage you get to rising commodity prices. As long as the gain in the price of the commodity the company produces outstrips any increase in their costs, you're laughing. When buying stock, you're also making an indirect bet on management—so nail the commodity and the management call, and you're sitting pretty. Best yet, many commodity producers are routinely able to build their reserves over time as they uncover more resources on the lands they lease. Buying commodity-producing equities allows you to prosper not only in the here and now as commodity prices improve, but also in the *future* as rising prices allow additional reserves to be discovered. Chosen prudently, commodity-producing equities can be a gift that keeps on giving.

In my career I've tried it all, and I keep coming back to a well-chosen basket of commodity-producing companies. With futures there's the "roll risk" to manage, plus a wide variety of new markets to study up on. Most commodity index funds are far too dependent on the shape of the curve to give you the kind of exposure you're looking for. For my money the choice is clear, commodity producers are the way for most investors to profit from a roaring commodity bull market.

$\sim$

A key benefit of buying the stocks of commodity-producing companies is the leverage you get to rising commodity prices.

Hot Commodities

- Owning your own oil field, mine, or farm is one way to get direct physical exposure to commodities, but it just isn't practical for most people.

- The price of a given futures contract will always converge to the "spot," or cash market price at expiration, but a lot can happen between the dates when futures contracts begin and expire.

- During the 1980s and 1990s, the futures curve for most commodities was downward sloping (backwardation), yet commodity funds were posting excellent results since they were able to buy low and sell high.

- Most stock indices are constructed and weighted according to the market capitalization of their components. In commodities, however, the concept of market capitalization doesn't apply.

- Commodity indices are often poor barometers for gauging activity levels in commodities.

- Commodity-producing companies offer leverage to rising commodity prices and the opportunity to benefit from reserve additions over time.

Gusher

Investing in Oil

No NATURAL RESOURCE IS MORE FIERCELY PRIZED or jealously guarded than oil. Ancient Egyptians used it for embalming and to support the walls of Babylon. Wars have been fought and empires created and destroyed in the epic conquest for the power and wealth that surrounds oil. Since 1854, when the kerosene lamp was invented, we've increased our dependence on the precious stuff and have sucked some 650 billion barrels of it from the ground. Access to abundant cheap oil makes suburbia and much of our modern world possible. Oil fuels our cars, planes, trains, and buses and is a critical feedstock for the plastics and cosmetics industries. Enough oil to fill a trillion barrels remains in the ground, but the cheap, easy-to-get stuff is already gone. As the world economy begins to grow after the global recession, oil prices will once again be heading higher. Much higher.

Big Oil

Everything about the oil business is big. Oil is the world's first trillion-dollar industry, it's the most actively traded commodity, and it's the single largest component of world trade. It's also the commodity that generates the most debate. Whether it's America's reliance on foreign imports, concern over your neighbor's carbon footprint, or the massive profits Big Oil (as the world's largest oil and gas manufacturers are collectively known) seems to be making when prices are moving higher—everyone has an opinion about oil.

To Err Is Human

Yet in spite of oil's importance to our way of life, publicly listed energy companies control just 15 percent of the world's known reserves. The rest are controlled by governments and their national oil companies, and many are less than friendly to the West. The poster boy for poor oil relations is Venezuela's Hugo Chávez, the left-leaning, anti-American leader who came to power in 1999. In May 2007, in his quest to make Venezuela into a socialist-inspired state, Chávez took dramatic action by stripping foreign oil companies of their majority interests in domestic oil fields. By mandating that state-controlled Petroleos de Venezuela (PDVSA) had to have at least 60 percent ownership in these new so-called "joint ventures," companies such as ExxonMobil, Chevron, and Total effectively had the rug pulled out from under them.

Publicly listed energy companies control just 15 percent of the world's known oil reserves.

But lately, with oil prices plunging from their previously lofty peaks, Chávez is humming a different tune. Once again he's soliciting bids from big Western oil companies—including many of those whose agreements he trampled on in 2007. Chávez needs Western money and know-how to unlock his vast reserves, yet he still holds most of the cards because Western oil companies are desperate to find large-scale projects in which to invest. As a result, once-spurned Western companies are still willing to take their chances on Venezuela. Talk about desperation!

Oil revenues account for about 93 percent of Venezuela's export revenue. And with the unpaid bills starting to stack up for social welfare programs such as health care and higher education, embracing Western oil companies may be Chávez's best option for balancing the books. The deal may be bad and the slice of the pie may be shrinking, but Venezuela—unlike other oil-rich countries where the national companies have a stranglehold on production—is at least willing to let multinational companies participate in the drilling. Saudi Arabia, the world's largest producer of crude oil, and Mexico have barred American and other foreign businesses from participating in the search for oil for more than half a century.

From Russia with Love

In Russia, the world's second largest producer of oil, muscle-flexing is the norm. For years, the Kremlin has moved aggressively to reclaim ownership of Russia's oil and gas industry from private firms. At one time, Yukos was Russia's largest private oil and gas company, worth an estimated $40 billion. But a personal rivalry with Vladimir Putin cost Yukos founder Mikhail Khodorkovsky, one of the notorious so-called Russian oligarchs, both his company and his freedom. For years, the Kremlin and the oligarchs had maintained an informal, mutually beneficial arrangement: the oligarchs would stay out of politics in exchange for the Kremlin keeping its nose out of the dubious circumstances under which this gang of fabulously wealthy businessmen gained control of former state assets. By Putin's second term as Russia's president, however, Khodorkovsky had soured on the arrangement and started funding opposition parties in the Duma. For Putin, this was intolerable. On October 25, 2003, Khodorkovsky, the wealthiest man in Russia at the time, was arrested and charged with fraud. Six days later, the Russian government froze trading in the shares of Yukos and brought charges of income tax evasion against the firm. In May 2005, Khodorkovsky was found guilty of fraud and sentenced to nine years in prison. With this criminal prosecution and the drawn-out dismantling of the company, an unequivocal message had been sent: *don't cross the Kremlin.*

In 2003, BP, one of the world's largest energy companies, acquired a 50 percent stake in one of Russia's largest oil companies, TNK. The joint venture, called TNK-BP, had President Putin's personal blessing. But the happy marriage didn't last long. Faster than you could say "oligarch," BP and the four Russian billionaires who shared control of Russia's third largest oil company had a falling out. The Russian partners took objection to TNK-BP's American chief executive, Robert Dudley, accusing him of favoring BP and running the joint venture like a subsidiary.

In a deal hammered out in September 2008, BP ceded to all the Russian partners' demands. BP agreed to dismiss Robert Dudley and appoint a Russian-speaking chief executive agreeable to its four major Russian shareholders. BP also agreed to create three additional independent seats on the board of directors. While it must have been a bitter pill for BP to swallow, it helped the company preserve its ownership interest in the joint venture, and with it, access to the large oil fields of Siberia. At a time when oil companies are struggling to find new reserves, a deal that permitted BP to preserve a quarter of its worldwide production was one it had to make.

While political risk may be part of the game for international oil and gas companies, it doesn't have to be a gamble that individual investors take. For my money, I prefer to bet on companies whose only risk is geological rather than political. Investing can be tricky enough without having to consult the minutes of the last UN meeting to try and figure out which way the political wind is blowing.

Have We Reached the Peak?

No debate is more contentious in the world of oil than the debate over whether or not the world has passed the peak of maximum oil production. The theory now known as "peak oil" was first advanced by Dr. M. King Hubbert, a geophysicist who worked for Shell Oil Company from 1943 to 1964. During his career, Hubbert made many significant contributions to the field of geophysics, but his most famous theory was that the rate of oil production for any given geography—be it an oil field, a nation, or the planet—would always resemble a bell curve. As time went by, production would increase until it hit its maximum or "peak" production, after which production would forever fall.

Hubbert first presented this theory, later dubbed the "Hubbert Curve," at a 1956 meeting of the American Petroleum Institute in San Antonio, Texas. He predicted that the United States would see oil production peak somewhere between the late 1960s and the early 1970s and thereafter enter an irrevocable decline in the lower 48 states. At the time, he was derided by colleagues who pointed out that all predictions made about oil capacity over the past half century had proven false. So when U.S. petroleum production peaked in 1970, as Hubbert had accurately predicted 14 years earlier, you can guess who had the last laugh.

~

When U.S. petroleum production peaked in 1970, as Hubbert had accurately predicted 14 years earlier, you can guess who had the last laugh.

According to the International Energy Agency's (IEA) report *World Energy Outlook 2008*, production from currently producing fields was set to start declining in 2009. The shortfall between the amount of oil that the Paris-based IEA figures the planet will need and what is currently being produced will have to come from yet-to-be-discovered oil fields, fields already discovered but not yet in production, natural gas liquids (NGLs), and non-conventional sources such as Canada's oil sands. NGLs are liquids such as propane, butane, and pentane, which are often found in oil reservoirs. While NGLs can be used in many chemical processes, such as the manufacturing of plastics, they aren't much good as fuel for your car. Over the next few decades, with the world's existing oil fields tired and their production in decline, the oil industry clearly faces a monumental task: finding vast, economically viable new reserves to exploit.

Hope Springs Eternal

Already, many of our most promising supply basins have rolled over and started to decline. The North Sea is case in point. Its two massive oil fields, the Forties and the Brent, were discovered in 1970 and 1971 respectively. The Forties field hit its peak production of 523,000 barrels per day in 1980, while the Brent hit its maximum of 440,000 barrels per day in 1985. In an effort to keep producing as much as possible for as long as possible, exploration and production companies injected massive amounts of water into the reservoirs in an attempt to sweep oil from the edges to the center, where it could be brought to the surface and collected more easily. By 2000, however, production from the North Sea had dropped like a stone, aggressive water flooding having ultimately exacerbated its decline.

The last major oil field to come into production was the giant Cantarell field in Mexico, which was discovered in 1975. With peak production of more than two million barrels a day, this was truly a Goliath of a field. To keep the good times rolling and boost production levels, Pemex, Mexico's national oil company, initiated an enhanced oil recovery program in 1998. Despite spending more than $10 billion on the effort, Cantarell's production started dropping quickly in 2003.

Shifting Sands

In 2007, when I visited the mammoth Syncrude project near Fort McMurray, Alberta, in the heart of Canada's oil sands, I felt as if I was standing on the surface of the moon. The earth had been scarred and was riddled with pockmarks; years of surface mining had altered the landscape forever. In the distance, I could see a small yellow dump truck. As it closed the nearly 30-mile (48 kilometer) distance to where I was standing, it became apparent that this was no ordinary dump truck. Rather, it was a massive Caterpillar 797 haul truck boasting a payload of 400 short tons and standing more than 50 feet (15 meters) high.

Projects such as Syncrude's are what the IEA hopes will become the cornerstone of future oil supply growth. Canada's oil sands reserves are massive, ranked a close second behind Saudi Arabia. However, getting all that gooey, sandy oil out of the ground and to market is no easy task. It requires either an enormous surface mining operation, or, when the resource is buried too far below the earth's surface, a highly energy-intensive operation involving the injection of steam into the reservoir to get the tar-like resource flowing. Once the oil is recovered, sand and impurities need to be removed and the oil upgraded before it can be sent by pipeline to refineries throughout North America. While the oil sands are a tremendous resource, removing oil from sand isn't cheap.

Decline

To hold oil production at 2008 levels, the global oil industry needs to find more than four million barrels per day—an amount equal to Iran's total 2008 production—each and every year. In 2008, the average oil field saw production declines of around 9.7 percent. By spending more than $250 billion annually on water flooding and other enhanced oil recovery techniques, the oil industry was able to slow the rate of decline to 5.1 percent per year.

———————————— ∽ ————————————

To hold oil production at 2008 levels, the global oil industry needs to find more than four million barrels per day of production—an amount equal to Iran's 2008 production—each and every year.

To find the huge new oil fields they require, exploration companies need to be drilling plenty of new exploration wells. Unfortunately, energy investment has slumped since 2008, as the effects of the global financial crisis made it harder for energy companies to secure the necessary financing. According to the IEA, global exploration spending plunged by over $90 billion, more than 19 percent, in 2009—the first such drop in more than a decade.

While exploration efforts remain muted, oil demand is forecast to soar as consumption in China and India increases. The IEA predicts that between now and 2030, fully 93 percent of the increase in overall energy demand will be driven by non-OECD* countries, with China and

* The Organisation for Economic Co-operation and Development (OECD) is a Paris-based organization that is one of the world's largest providers of economic research. Its member countries are developed nations committed to democracy and to a market economy.

India alone accounting for 53 percent of future demand. Not only must new oil fields be found to make up for dwindling production from existing fields, but the IEA also estimates that at least 20 million barrels per day of *additional* production will need to be found over the next 20 years. Good luck!

For Big Oil, a perfect storm of slumping global supplies, voracious demand, and increasingly hostile host governments have made it difficult to grow its "reserve base"—that is, the inventory from which oil companies produce their supply each year. For the large major producers, the lack of access to quality projects and the high cost of finding and booking reserves have left them in a difficult position. In 2008, the average reserve life (reserves/current annual production) for the six largest publicly listed oil companies, or "super majors," was just 12.2 years. At current rates of production, and in the absence of new discoveries, the super majors will be out of oil reserves in less than 15 years.

At current rates of production, and without new discoveries, the super majors will be out of oil reserves in less than 15 years.

That Great Sucking Sound

Big Oil has found itself trapped between a rock and a hard place. Shareholders are demanding increases in both production and reserves, yet Western oil companies are often stymied in their quest for new oil. Increasingly, companies are investing billions in cutting-edge technologies to unlock more of the oil that lies trapped below the earth's surface. But despite major advances in the industry over the last century, a shocking two-thirds of all oil still gets left in the ground.

Despite major advances in the oil industry over the last century, a shocking two-thirds of all oil still gets left in the ground.

If international oil companies can raise the recovery rates on existing oil fields from a paltry 35 percent to closer to 50 percent, the world's recoverable oil reserves would soar. The *Oil and Gas Journal,* a leading industry magazine, estimates that with current recovery rates, the world has 1.34 trillion barrels of recoverable oil reserves. At a 50 percent recovery rate, that number could zoom to a staggering 2.5 trillion barrels! So far, however, the dream of recovering vast new amounts of trapped oil has proved elusive.

Energy companies are constantly looking for new ways to unlock more oil. Water flooding is often used in aging reservoirs, while techniques such as nitrogen injection are used to thin and mobilize oil in much the same way that detergent cuts the grease on dinner plates. Yet in spite of all of these efforts, global recovery rates remain alarmingly low.

Second Coming?

While new oil fields are being discovered all the time, they are increasingly in remote, inhospitable parts of the world. The latest things to set hearts racing are the massive discoveries in Brazil, some 180 miles from the coast of Rio de Janeiro in the Santos Oil Basin. In all, three major new fields—the Tupi, Jupiter, and Sugar Loaf—have been found, comprising the largest oil discoveries since 2000. By some estimates, the three fields could contain as many as 80 billion barrels of oil, enough to launch Brazil into the big leagues of oil-producing and oil-exporting nations.

But there's a catch. The fields lie in ultra deep water, more than 2.5 miles below the seabed. And a bigger problem is that these fields are located in the ocean's pre-salt layer, which makes drilling for oil extremely difficult and expensive. The Tupi field alone could cost in excess of $600 billion to develop. Collectively, the major fields in the Santos Basin will cost in excess of $1.5 trillion to bring into full production—a hefty price tag.

Fill 'Er Up

Demand for oil is also expected to grow in the very same part of the world that we'll be looking to for future oil supplies: the Middle East. Outside of Asia, the Middle East is showing the fastest rate of increase in demand, accounting for roughly 10 percent of the incremental global energy demand forecasted by the IEA.

One reason for this increased demand is heavy sub-sidization at Middle Eastern gas pumps. While we start to grumble pretty loudly when the cost of topping up our tanks hits $4 per gallon, many of our pals in Saudi Arabia are paying a mere 45 cents per gallon. And while it's cheap to drive in the Middle East, operating a cab in Caracas, Venezuela, has got to be the best deal going. Gasoline prices in Chávez's Soviet-styled state clocked in at a jaw-dropping 17 cents per gallon in 2008. Oil subsidies are a big deal throughout most of the oil-producing world. According to the IEA, the 20 largest non-OECD energy-consuming countries spent an estimated $150 bil-lion on subsidies in 2007. An afternoon spin is a lot more fun when someone else is footing the bill!

Nice Wheels

In the U.S., vehicle sales fell 18 percent during 2008. In China, however, they continued to climb despite the worldwide recession. In the last decade alone, car sales in China have surged fivefold, leaving foreign manufacturers, such as General Motors Corp. and Volkswagen AG, and their Chinese partners scrambling to produce enough cars to meet the demand. In February of 2009, the manufacturers' hard work paid off, as the sale of vehicles in China surpassed those of the U.S. for the first time.

In August of 2009, China achieved yet another economic milestone when it became the largest car manufacturing nation on the planet, despite the fact that it did not export a single car. India's Tata Motors, owner of the Jaguar and Range Rover brands, has begun to produce an entry-level car called the Nano, which retails for just $2,000. With a sticker price that low, more drivers are bound to be hitting the roads in India and China, which can only mean one thing: higher gasoline prices for North Americans.

Crack Shack

Refiners are a key component of the oil and gas business, and yet they often get short shrift. In the business, the joke is that refiners are the "commodities' commodity." Refinery guys were always the ones wearing the chocolate

brown suits and thick-soled loafers at the oil and gas conferences. The business, while complex and indispensible,
just isn't all that sexy or profitable. Whether they're
stand-alone independents or part of integrated oil and gas
companies, refiners are price takers. Their profitability
lies in the razor-thin margins between what they get for
selling refined products, such as gasoline, diesel, and fuel
oil, and the costs of buying the crude oil from producers.

Today, with crude prices high and gasoline storage
full, American refineries are getting squeezed on all
sides. Adding to their misery is the fact that the crude oil
they're receiving is increasingly both sour (high in sulfur
content) and heavy (doesn't flow easily). Most refineries in
the U.S. were developed in an era when the light, sweet
blend of crude oil (the type that the WTI contract is
based on) was the norm. But today, as the oil fields have
aged and production is starting to get a little long in the
tooth, light, sweet crude oil makes up just 15 percent of
the global crude slate. And that means costly retrofits (in
the billions of dollars per refinery) to rearrange the various pots and pans necessary to handle the heavier sour
grades of crude that have become so prevalent.

With America awash in gasoline and refineries working
at just 80 percent capacity utilization, the stock market
has sold off the shares of the independent refining companies. Refiners make their highest margin selling lighter,

more valuable products such as gasoline. To produce gasoline from crude oil, the oil molecules first need to be "cracked" in devices such as hydrocrackers or fluid catalytic crackers. The profit margin that refiners make in the process is thus known as the "crack spread." Today, the crack spread has collapsed from a high of $31.98 per barrel on December 31, 1998, to around $7 per barrel—a loss of more than 70 percent.

The profit margin that refiners make in upgrading crude oil to products such as gasoline is known as the *crack spread*.

Slick Operators

Once upon a time, billions of dollars were chasing Internet stocks, but today the hot money is flowing into oil and commodity funds. Unlike the Internet investment fad, this bull market is underpinned by some pretty solid fundamentals: namely, sagging supply and soaring demand. And that's making a lot of people in London and New York rich.

As a critical feedstock for the modern economy, oil is quite simply the most visible and important of all the traded commodities. This is reflected on the trading floor at NYMEX, where oil is traded alongside natural gas, coffee, and copper by brokers who buy and sell contracts to deliver these goods for a certain price at a future date. Unlike the modern, computerized trading platforms such as NASDAQ, the NYMEX is an open-outcry system where, depending on the commodity, floor traders meet in preassigned circular pits to match buy and sell orders from the marketplace. When I visited the floor, it was a maze of activity, with phone cables everywhere, runners going every which way, and traders shouting at the top of their lungs. But no pit was as physically large, boisterous, or action-packed as the crude oil pit, where floor traders were executing client orders from around the world.

Far away from the testosterone-fueled trading floor of the NYMEX sit the *really* slick operators in the world of oil trading: the commodity traders employed by hedge funds and investment banks. Here, an unexpected calm reigns as billions of dollars are wagered on the spread between light, sweet crude, and heavy crude oil prices. Trades are executed in the blink of an eye by a bank of computers reacting to preset trading algorithms or by traders with advanced degrees in mathematics. As commodity prices move higher, the demand for trading talent has increased dramatically. Today, a decent mid-level trader who knows the energy complex well can easily earn between $1 and $3 million per year—a level once reserved for the top traders.

Nowadays, oil traders aren't just buying contracts for the future delivery of oil, they're also chartering super-tankers to *store* the crude in the hope of reselling it for a profit months later. And in what's been dubbed the "trade of the year," companies such as Citigroup and Morgan Stanley have been snapping up this floating storage at deeply discounted rates. In 2008, when rental rates plunged 78 percent, some savvy traders secured 7 percent of the global fleet of large crude carriers.

Petrol Profits

As the global economy begins to grow again, oil prices will head higher. Strong demand, sluggish supply, and technical and operational challenges will continue to plague the industry, making higher oil prices a foregone conclusion. Investors looking to profit from the coming bull market in petroleum need look no further than the stocks of well-run oil and gas companies engaged in exploration and production activities. Companies with long-lived oil reserves in countries with low political risk should be the go-to names for investors looking to pump up their profits.

—————————— ∼ ——————————

Companies with long-lived oil reserves in countries with low political risk should be the go-to names for investors looking to pump up their profits.

Big Oil, with its short reserve lives and narrowing slate of international opportunities, will underperform the exploration and production companies in the oil run-up. But if the market heads south in a hurry, as it did in 2008, large capitalization companies such as ExxonMobil will be the place to ride out the storm. Refiners and integrated oil and gas companies will continue to be laggards for the foreseeable future as low margins in the refining business will continue to act as a damper on stock prices.

Hot Commodities

- No commodity is more visible, important, controversial, or crucial to our modern way of life than oil.
- Publicly listed energy companies control just 15 percent of the world's known oil reserves.
- With the world's existing oil fields tired and in decline, the industry will face the monumental task of finding vast, economically viable new reserves to exploit over the next few decades.

(continued)

- To hold global oil production at 2008 levels, the industry needs to find supply equal to that currently produced by Iran—each and every year.

- The IEA predicts that between now and 2030, the lion's share of demand (93 percent) will be driven by non-OECD countries, with China and India alone accounting for 53 percent of this figure.

- A perfect storm of slumping global supplies, voracious demand, and increasingly hostile host governments has made it difficult for Big Oil to grow their reserve bases.

- Despite major advances in the industry over the last century, more than two-thirds of all oil still gets left in the ground.

- The profit margin created when refiners upgrade crude oil to products such as gasoline is known as the "crack spread."

- Companies with long-lived oil reserves in countries with low political risk should be the go-to investments for those looking to pump up their profits.

- Refiners and integrated oil and gas companies will continue to be laggards for the foreseeable future, as low margins in the refining business continue to act as a damper on stock prices.

Chapter Four

Drilling for Dollars

~

Profiting from Natural Gas

NATURAL GAS HAS A LOT GOING FOR IT. It's clean burning, cheaper than oil, and a low carbon fuel—making it a great choice in these environmentally conscious times. Nearly 20 percent of America's power plants burn natural gas, and these plants can be constructed in a jiffy, making them a sensible alternative to coal plants. Better still, natural-gas-fired power plants produce just half the carbon dioxide that similarly sized coal plants do—a very big plus when you consider that electricity generation is *the* biggest source of greenhouse gas emissions. Yet in spite of all these advantages, natural gas has one big weakness for commodity investors: it's abundant.

Be Careful What You Wish For

Between 2005 and 2008, however, the worry was just the opposite—a dramatic shortage of natural gas in North America. With Mexican imports falling and Canadian supply barely staying level, America needed more natural gas and it needed it in a hurry. Lack of supply led to concerns about what would happen if a massive category five hurricane ripped through the Gulf of Mexico, causing producers to shut in much needed capacity. And what if other weather extremes forced a blazing hot summer or frigid winter upon us at the exact same time that gas production was struggling? Suddenly, drilling rigs were being contracted at a furious pace, and gas producers were sucking as much gas as they could from the ground.

As concerns mounted, pipeline companies and entrepreneurs started proposing new natural gas terminals that could receive gas from abroad in liquefied form. But to get gas to America from Qatar, Trinidad, or wherever it was for sale, it would first have to be supercooled to minus 260 degrees Fahrenheit (minus 162 degrees Celsius), compressed to one six-hundredth its original volume, turned into a liquid (liquefied natural gas or LNG), and placed onto specially designed, double-hulled ships.

New receiving terminals would need to be built throughout North America to convert the LNG back into a gas so it could be sent by pipeline to the utilities and industries that needed it most.

With the market abuzz about yet another hurricane barreling towards the Gulf, natural gas prices peaked on December 15, 2005, at $15.38 per thousand cubic feet—a price roughly equivalent to $92.27 per barrel of oil. Suddenly, the tables had turned. Natural gas, a product once considered an annoying nuisance by the oil industry, was now very much in demand, having seen a spectacular fourteenfold increase in value from January 2002—just three short years earlier.

From Import Terminals to Airport Terminals

In 2007, with gas prices once again hitting all-time highs and existing natural gas fields showing average production declines of about 15 percent per year, more gas needed to be found. For a long time, geologists had known that massive shale gas formations existed throughout North America, but the cost of getting commercial quantities of gas from the shale was prohibitive. Everything changed, however, when some enterprising oil and gas men from Texas started experimenting with a couple of new technologies in the Barnett Shale under the Dallas/Fort Worth Airport.

Horizontal drilling was the first thing they tried. Instead of drilling straight down into the resource, they tried drilling down and then sideways to open up a larger area of the underground formation. But to really liberate the trapped gas they needed a way to move it towards the surface. So, next on the list was a technique called hydraulic fracturing—or "fraccing"—where water and sand are injected under high pressure into the reservoir, resulting in many tiny cracks or fractures in the shale rock. Combining these two techniques produced the most dramatic results. In addition to producing more than 160 trillion cubic feet (Tcf) of natural gas between 2000 and 2008, proven natural gas reserves in the U.S. grew to 245 Tcf, up from just 177 Tcf in 2000.

This potent combination of horizontal drilling and fraccing has revolutionized the North American natural gas business. In 1990, gas from unconventional reservoirs such as shale rock, so-called "tight" formations, and the seams of coal beds made up just 10 percent of total U.S. production. Today, new shale plays, as they are often called, appear to be popping up just about everywhere, accounting for 40 percent of U.S. production and making unconventional gas drilling the place to be.

Natural gas storage is also bursting at the seams. *Everybody* thought gas prices were going to go higher, instead they slumped as technology unleashed massive quantities of shale gas that had previously been locked under the earth's surface. The conventional drilling rigs that once dotted the landscape in West Texas lie idle, having been replaced with new-fangled pressure pumping equipment. According to the Baker Hughes rig count, an important barometer of oil field service activity, there were approximately 2,300 drilling rigs active in North America by the end of 2008. A year later, that number had slumped to around 1,400—a nearly 40 percent drop. Low gas prices and technological innovation have changed the conventional drilling world forever.

Weather Bets

When I used to take visitors around the Enron trading floor in downtown Houston, Texas, I often got the same response: "What? You guys have nothing better to do than watch the weather channel?" Little did these visitors know that weather explained somewhere between 50 to 80 percent of the price of natural gas. Unlike oil, which is used primarily as a transportation fuel, natural gas is used for heating and cooling, as well as by industry. In summertime, natural gas-fired electricity plants help keep our air conditioning running flat-out, and in winter, gas is used to heat our homes and businesses.

---— ⁓ ---—

Weather explains somewhere between 50 to 80 percent of the price of natural gas.

While ignorance may be bliss, it sure as heck isn't profitable. The sharks who traded for keeps at Enron knew that nothing would get gas prices moving more quickly than rumors of a fast-moving hurricane in the Gulf of Mexico that had managed to shutter half of the natural gas rigs in the area. Whether the rumor was real or just *convenient* didn't matter. Gas prices, which are more volatile than oil prices, were going to be on the move regardless—and that would mean fat profits for the trader on the right side of the weather bet.

---— ⁓ ---—

Natural gas prices are more volatile than oil prices.

To get an edge on the competition, savvy gas traders study everything from the amount of volcanic ash in the atmosphere to the water temperatures in the Gulf of Mexico. But one bet that is sure to be profitable is that winter gas prices will always be higher than summer prices, especially when it's freezing cold in the U.S. Northeast and storage levels are low.

Back when Enron was still a going concern, they were structuring all kinds of products for large buyers of natural gas—such as local gas-distribution companies—to help offer price protection from rising gas prices in the months of October to March. In the summer, exploration and production companies were looking to lock-in a bottom for gas prices to protect their profits should gas prices take a tumble—and Enron was only too willing to help.

A Pipeline of Profits

With its seasonal pricing patterns and enough variables and volatility to leave you with worse whiplash than a high-speed collision, natural gas futures trading is a potential bonanza for savvy traders. For energy trader John Arnold, a numbers whiz on Enron's natural gas desk, the complexity of trading natural gas was second nature. After the firm's collapse, Arnold, then 28 years old, decided to take some of his 2001 year-end bonus of $8 million and create his own energy trading hedge fund: Centaurus Advisors. So far, it's been a good move. Since the fund's inception in 2002, Arnold has returned at least 80 percent every year—making him one of America's youngest billionaires, with an estimated net worth of $1.5 billion.

For those not so nimble, the volatile, high-stakes business of natural gas trading can exact a painful toll.

One former wunderkind who found himself on the wrong side of Arnold's trades was former Amaranth Advisors natural gas trader Brian Hunter. For a while, Hunter seemed to be able to do no wrong. After earning a master's degree in mathematics from the University of Alberta and working a short stint at TransCanada Corp., a pipeline company based in Calgary, Alberta, Hunter headed south to New York City. He landed a job at Deutsche Bank in May 2001. In his first two years he made over $69 million for the bank, and was soon promoted to head its natural gas trading desk. Not satisfied with the sleepy world of natural gas trading at an investment bank, Hunter was lured away by the big money promises of Amaranth Advisors founder Nick Maounis, who wanted a star natural gas trader in his lineup.

Maounis's gamble in hiring Hunter, who earlier had sued Deutsche Bank over a withheld bonus, seemed to be paying off. Hunter solidified his reputation as a rising star during 2005, when he bet the right way on natural gas prices after Hurricanes Katrina and Rita ripped through the U.S. Gulf Coast, making a boatload of profits for Amaranth in the process.

After posting such big gains in 2005, Hunter was given more latitude to control his own trades through Amaranth's Greenwich, Connecticut, trading floor—no longer having to pre-clear them before execution. He was named co-head of the firm's energy desk and allowed to operate from Calgary, rather than from Connecticut. Unfortunately for Amaranth, the increased personal latitude they extended to Hunter proved to be ill-fated. A year and a half later, the company imploded with losses of approximately $6 billion on natural gas bets gone bad—a staggering sum for a firm with just $9 billion in assets.

A lack of proper trading oversight, enormous leverage, faulty judgment, and poor risk management practices created the perfect storm of problems that led to Amaranth's dissolution in October of 2006. Traders such as Hunter could employ tremendous leverage to magnify both their gains and their losses. In trading natural gas futures on organized exchanges such as the NYMEX, traders often had to post collateral of only 10 percent of their total position. Small percentage moves in the price for natural gas can have a dramatic impact on traders who are not fully collateralized, and when combined with generous lines of credit from banks, commodity hedge funds can fast become heavily leveraged.

Small percentage moves in the price for natural gas can have a dramatic impact on traders who are not fully collateralized.

When the end came for Amaranth, it came quickly. Hunter placed bets in 2006 that would pay off exponentially for the firm if, and *only* if, future gas prices moved sharply higher. This time, he was betting on the prospect that a nasty hurricane or cold winter would hit natural gas facilities, sending March futures prices higher. As September dragged on and the evidence began to accumulate that not only would the winter be mild, but that the hurricane season would also be a non-event, natural gas prices fell. Brian Hunter's disastrous weather bet was more than enough to cripple Amaranth. Taking the opposing view to Hunter was none other than John Arnold, who managed to have one of his best years ever in 2007, after he bet that winter gas prices would *fall* rather than rise. Arnold's weather bet was a winner—his fund was up over 200 percent that year.

Methane Man

As I sat within a large semicircle at the Bank of America hedge fund conference in Dallas, a hush descended over the crowd. As T. Boone Pickens began to speak, everyone's eyes were glued on the legend—a courtly, dignified southern gentleman. He talked about his plans for his new company, a hedge fund called BP Capital Management.

To say that T. Boone Pickens has led a colorful life is an understatement. After graduating from Oklahoma

A&M in 1951, Pickens worked for Phillips Petroleum before venturing out on his own as a wildcatter in search of oil. He later founded a firm called Mesa Petroleum and, through acquisitions, grew it to become one of the largest independent oil companies in the world. During the 1980s, he led a string of takeovers and attempted buyouts of undervalued oil and gas companies including Cities Service, Phillips Petroleum, Gulf Oil, and Unocal. Since most of his deals were never completed, Pickens gained a reputation as a corporate raider and greenmailer, but that turned out not to matter, since the mere disclosure that he had acquired a substantial stake in a company was enough to send its stock price soaring. Along the way, Pickens has accumulated a personal fortune of approximately $3 billion and is currently ranked by Forbes as the 117th richest person in America.

Today, Pickens is known as much for his activism as for his gutsy investments. He believes that oil has entered a period of irrevocable decline and that America needs to find alternative fuels for transportation. His solution, the Pickens Plan, aims to end America's addiction to foreign oil by replacing it with natural gas. And after investing $58 million in a series of television advertisements and YouTube videos, he's finally managed to get people talking about the possibility of fueling cars with compressed natural gas.

Gas Glut

Oil and natural gas used to trade in tandem. The reason was simple: the heat content, or British Thermal Unit (BTU), of a thousand cubic feet of natural gas was approximately one-sixth of that contained in one barrel of oil. If natural gas was going for $4 per thousand cubic feet and oil was trading for $24 per barrel (4x6 = $24 on an energy equivalent basis), then all was as it should be in the world of energy. If oil was trading for $40 per barrel and natural gas for $3 per thousand cubic feet, then the old logic was that power plants burning #2 or #6 fuel oil could switch over to natural gas to take advantage of the price discrepancy between the two fuels. In time, as more power plants made the switch from oil to natural gas, the price differential would eventually close. Or so the logic went.

But the problem with that logic is that oil is a global commodity whose price is set by supply and demand the world over. On the other hand, because natural gas must be transported to the market by pipeline, it's more likely to be impacted by local supply and demand factors. The price of natural gas in Japan or Russia has limited impact on the price of gas in America.

~

**Oil is a global commodity, but natural gas is
priced and traded regionally.**

Breaking Up Is Hard to Do

Old habits die hard. Throughout most of 2009, as oil prices moved up from $35 to close to $80 per barrel and natural gas prices remained stuck at $4 per thousand cubic feet, many investors sensed an opportunity. Surely, they reasoned, with oil and gas now trading at a ratio of 20:1—instead of the historical 6:1—there were some easy profits to be made.

To capitalize on this apparent anomaly, many retail investors piled into exchanged traded funds (ETFs) linked to natural gas, reasoning that the funds would do a good job of tracking the current price of gas. Unfortunately, they were misguided. Most single-commodity ETFs buy futures contracts, which are bets on the price of a commodity at a *future* date. The problem is, the futures contracts that the ETFs buy sometimes do a bad job of tracking the price of the commodity in the here and now (also known as the spot price).

A case in point was United States Natural Gas Fund (UNG—NYSE), a single-commodity ETF linked to natural gas. Buoyed by the logic that oil and gas prices would eventually have to converge on their historical trading relationship, investors started buying up units of UNG. From the beginning of 2009 through mid-year, the fund attracted some $4 billion of new investor money—a dramatic increase in assets from the $300 million the fund had in December of 2008. So much investor money was flowing into UNG that it was becoming a dominant force in the market for natural gas futures. To prevent the fund from having undue influence on the natural gas futures market, U.S. regulators temporarily banned it from issuing new units.

While futures prices are generally a good proxy for what commodity prices are doing in the here and now, this isn't always the case. Unfortunately for investors in UNG, 2009 turned out to be a disappointing year. Not only did oil and natural gas prices decouple from their historical trading ratio, but mild weather and slumping demand increased investors' pain by causing natural gas prices to fall further. Making matters worse, while natural gas prices tumbled approximately 38 percent in the first 11 months of 2009, units in UNG tumbled more than 60 percent, a reflection of the difference between futures prices and spot prices.

Drilling for Dollars

With plenty of natural gas available from shale formations and natural gas storage facilities stuffed to the brim, it may be a while before gas prices start shooting higher. But because natural gas prices are so dependent on weather, a frigid winter or boiling hot summer could be just what's needed to get gas prices moving higher again.

Big-name traders may subscribe to a wide variety of newsletters written by experts purporting to be able to accurately forecast the weather, but for most of us this approach is a waste of time. Proper weather forecasting is made up of such a dizzying array of variables that no software program I am aware of can accurately predict *tomorrow's* weather, let alone get it right several months or years in advance. Blowing your hard-earned money on weather forecasts to try to get a handle on the natural gas market is like consulting the psychic hotline about your love life—it's a complete waste of time. A better bet is to consult the Weekly Natural Gas Storage Report (available at www.eia.doe.gov) put out by the Energy Information Administration (EIA), part of the Department of Energy, to get a sense of the amount of natural gas in storage (a measure of natural gas inventory) and how it compares to five-year average storage levels. Given that most U.S. utilities are mandated by law to have enough natural gas to meet worst-case demand levels, it's a pretty good bet that gas prices will head sharply higher if storage levels are near empty.

Since close to 80 percent of all drilling activity in the lower 48 states and Western Canada is tied to natural gas drilling, it also makes sense to keep track of the number of drilling rigs working at any one time. The Baker Hughes rig count (available at www.bakerhughesdirect. com) is a widely followed barometer of what is going on in the field. If it shows that more drilling rigs are being contracted out at ever increasing day rates, you can be sure that the professionals running the nation's oil and gas firms believe that, over the long term, natural gas prices are heading higher.

As oil and gas firms evolved, they gradually contracted out their drilling teams and other service professionals in an attempt to shed some of their fixed costs. Today, drilling companies operate in much the same way that consultants operate—on a fee-for-service basis. When the natural gas market is on fire, the drilling companies are working flat out. But once gas prices start to tumble, the first thing that exploration and production companies do is slash their drilling budget. As a result, the stock prices of drilling companies tend to be even more volatile than those of producing companies. When investors sense that natural gas prices are about to move sharply higher, buying shares in a good quality drilling company is a wise bet.

Once natural gas prices start to move out of the basement again, the producing companies who have dominant land positions, solid balance sheets, and first-class management teams will be the likely winners. One company that fits the bill is Encana Corporation (ECA—NYSE), which has done a marvelous job of protecting its cash flows by locking in favorable gas prices (hedging) at opportune times. Not only that, but Encana was accumulating dominant land positions in some of the best shale formations throughout North America long before it was fashionable.

While gas prices have dropped lately, all it will take to get them moving higher again is a wave of industry consolidation, or an extreme and long-lasting bout of nasty weather. Without a doubt, the historical trading ratio between oil and gas is all but dead. But gas will once again have its day, and when it does, the service companies that specialize in fraccing shale rock, the drillers who can make their drill bits move both down *and* sideways, and the producers who have the best land positions and lowest cost structures will come out ahead.

Hot Commodities

- By combining horizontal drilling and hydraulic fraccing techniques, massive new gas fields can be developed—a game changer for the natural gas business.

- There is a surplus of natural gas in North America, which has depressed gas prices.

- Natural gas prices are more volatile than oil prices.

- Somewhere between 50 to 80 percent of the variability in natural gas prices can be explained by the weather. This relationship is stronger in the winter months.

- Oil prices have become decoupled from natural gas prices and the historical trading ratio of 6:1 no longer applies.

- The Baker Hughes rig count is a decent leading indicator of overall oil field and service activity.

- The U.S. Department of Energy issues weekly gas storage reports that can help investors gauge the amount of natural gas in inventory.

- When natural gas prices recover, the best bets for investment are likely to be in the service companies that specialize in horizontal drilling and reservoir fraccing, and in the producers that specialize in developing the so-called unconventional gas reservoirs.

Chapter Five

Going for Gold

Prospering with Gold and Precious Metals

FEW SUBJECTS IN THE WORLD OF INVESTING are as polarizing as gold. Its unique emotional lure, dating from ancient times, captures the imagination of investors the world over. To some, gold is a barbarous relic, to others, it's a currency whose time has come. Skeptics point out that, over the past 90 years, a bet on the Dow Jones Industrial Average would have won out over an investment in gold. But there is one thing everyone seems to agree on, and that's if there was ever a time for gold and precious metals to outperform all other assets: *this is it*.

A perfect storm is brewing that will likely lift gold and precious metal prices higher in the near term. Precious metals often outperform stocks, real estate, and bonds during times when banks are under stress and the U.S. dollar is weak. Add inflationary pressures into the mix and you've got the conditions for an explosive rally in precious metals. Investors are beginning to warm up to gold and precious metals as they survey the potholed road of governmental finances and conclude that the West is deeply in debt.

Gold and precious metals often outperform stocks, real estate, and bonds during times when banks are under stress, the U.S. dollar is weak, and inflation is running rampant.

Awash in Debt

During the global financial crisis of 2008–2009, Wall Street banks faced a near-death experience that left the survivors deeply indebted to government and wary of a wave of regulatory reform. Wall Street may have led the charge to government largesse, but others were quick to follow.

A lineup began to form around Capitol Hill, as everyone from auto executives to concerned citizens came to plead their case for a pocketful of government cash. In 2008 and 2009, the U.S. Federal Reserve pumped an additional $2 trillion into the American economy to help stimulate consumption. Unfortunately, this massive cash infusion didn't result in an uptick in GDP.

In December 2008, the U.S. Fed chopped its benchmark federal funds rate to near zero in the hope of resuscitating the American economy by stimulating spending with lots of cheap cash. But the average American consumer and business was still too petrified to spend, leaving the U.S. government itself as the main engine of economic growth during 2009. And spend they did. On February 1, 2010, U.S. President Barack Obama unveiled his $3.83 trillion budget, which projected a massive $1.56 trillion deficit for the fiscal year. Even more worrisome, the budget also projected that America would be saddled with trillion-dollar deficits for at least three years.

Even by the optimistic standards of an incumbent president presenting a budget to Congress, this document contained some stunning revelations. The most striking, buried deep within it, was that even by the government's own rosy economic projections, America's deficit would not return to what are widely considered sustainable levels until sometime around 2020. When that date begins to approach, increasing healthcare costs associated with retiring baby boomers will put upward pressure on the deficit, suggesting that even *this* budget may be wishful thinking. With its debt rising faster than its income, America is attempting to keep its head above water as the cost of servicing the nation's debt acts like an anchor, weighing down future economic growth.

Start the Presses

America is not alone with its fiscal problems. The United Kingdom, Greece, Spain, and many other countries have all suffered under the weight of massive debts as the bad habit of too much spending and not enough saving envelops most of the West. Faced with the prospect of sluggish economic growth, or worse, outright default on their debts, governments at home and abroad are all eyeing the printing press as a way out of their predicaments.

The value of the U.S. dollar, or any paper currency, is directly linked to the amount of currency in circulation at any one time. Increase the number of U.S. dollars in circulation and the value declines. Back in 2002, U.S. Federal Reserve Chairman Ben Bernanke said: "the U.S. government has a technology, called a printing press (or, today, its electronic equivalent), that allows it to produce as many U.S. dollars as it wishes at essentially no cost."

When their debts get out of hand, governments find it all too tempting to fire up the presses and flood the market with dollars. For politicians facing reelection, the choice between debasing the currency, imposing sky-high taxes, or implementing draconian cuts in services is a simple one. It's easiest to warm up the printing presses and trash the currency—something that savvy precious metals traders are all too happy to capitalize on.

Gold has proven reliable and durable for thousands of years, having outlasted every single paper currency the world has ever known. And because the supplies of gold and other precious metals are finite, central bankers can't inflate away their value. What's more, unlike financial assets, gold and precious metals are nobody else's liability. Venezuela is case in point. In January 2010, with the official inflation rate running at 27 percent, President Hugo Chávez decided to devalue the Venezuelan bolivar to stimulate exports and boost the country's economy. With the stroke of a pen, Chávez devalued the bolivar by half—from 2.15 to 4.30 per U.S. dollar—a move that effectively reduced the value of bolivar-denominated savings by half. Those Venezuelans lucky enough to have had significant holdings in gold or silver would have been safe from these drastic measures, since precious metals cannot be devalued overnight on the whim of a government leader.

A Golden Era

A golden era may be upon us as concern mounts over the monumental debt being racked up by the U.S. government. With the banking system in distress, inflation running amok, and the U.S. dollar in decline, gold is *the* go-to investment. Gold last peaked in 1980 at $850 per ounce, which, when adjusted for inflation, is the equivalent of $2,189 per ounce in 2009 dollars.

Gold last peaked in 1980 at $850 per ounce, which, when adjusted for inflation, is the equivalent of $2,189 per ounce in 2009 dollars.

When times are tough, people gravitate towards something tangible, something they can hold in their hands, like gold coins or bars. And lately, the demand for gold bullion (physical coins, ingots, and bars) has been high. According to the World Gold Council, retail demand for gold bullion zoomed in the fourth quarter of 2008, up nearly fivefold from the previous year. But bullion's zenith was during the early 1980s, when buying physical gold hit its peak.

The Golden Rules

Unlike paper money, gold supply is finite, making scarcity one of the big benefits of owning gold. Estimates have pegged the amount of gold above ground at around 165,000 metric tons, with some 20,000 metric tons still waiting to be mined. Nearly 90 percent of the known gold in the world, with a rough value of $4.5 trillion, has already been mined. That's a big number, yet it pales in comparison to the more than $8 trillion U.S. dollars in circulation and a world stock market capitalization of roughly $40 trillion. And stack gold up against the outstanding notional value of the world's derivatives market—a whopping $800 trillion—and the value of physical gold looks puny. In fact, the ratio of gold to paper currencies is currently at an *all-time low*, which suggests that the stage is being set for a powerful rally.

Nearly 90 percent of the known gold has been mined, with an approximate value of $4.5 trillion—a substantial sum, but it pales in comparison with those of paper-based assets. The global stock markets have a market capitalization of around $40 trillion, and the notional value of the outstanding derivative securities is a staggering $800 trillion.

The ancient Egyptians first mined gold in 2000 BC, but it was during the Roman Empire that it became prized for its beauty and scarcity. So rare is gold, that all the gold mined since it was first discovered would fill just two Olympic-sized swimming pools. Today, gold is most often used in jewelry (62 percent of consumption) or held by retail customers in bar and coin form. It's also held in vaults to backstop various investment products, most notably a wide range of gold ETFs, which accounts for around 9 percent of overall demand. Because it is non-corrosive and a good conductor of electricity, gold is used in a number of industrial applications, such as electronic circuitry.

South Africa was once gold's biggest producer, but today China has taken the lead—accounting for 13 percent of world supply. South Africa's production peaked in the 1970s, but now the country produces just half as much as it did back then. However, it still accounts for more than 10 percent of the world's mine supply of gold, while Australia and the United States round out the top four producing countries. Gold is found all over the world, but it's getting increasingly hard to find and more expensive to mine. The "grade," or percentage of gold in mineral-bearing rock (ore), has declined worldwide from an average of 9.6 grams (0.3 ounces) per metric ton in 1977 to just under 1.5 grams (0.05 ounces) per metric ton today. Gold mining is also the most waste-intensive of all mining operations. To produce enough gold for a single wedding ring, more than 250 metric tons of rock needs to be moved, crushed, and sorted. In spite of massive operations, the hunt for gold is proving increasingly difficult. Between 2003 and 2008, total global mine production fell at an average rate of 1.1 percent per year.

Money in the Bank

The stage has been set for higher gold prices, yet gold's fundamentals are still the weakest of all the metals. Conventional explanations of supply and demand ring a little hollow when it comes to gold. For starters, all the gold ever mined is still in existence—as jewelry and coins, or tucked away in central bank vaults. During the 1990s, when commodity prices slumped and miners abandoned the search for copper and other base metals, gold exploration continued to represent almost 60 percent of all mining projects. Gold demand is driven largely by fickle jewelry buyers and investment flows, both of which are hard to predict. Supply is made up of mine output, inventory coming back on the market from central banks, and recycled gold.

Of course, so-called gold bugs don't like it pointed out that the 3,600 metric tons of annual gold demand can only be met by smelting down your grandmother's jewelry.

Recycled gold represents around 24 percent of the metal's annual supply, while mine production accounts for about 68 percent. To keep market shocks to a minimum and to provide a balance between supply and demand, the central banks function as virtual gold mines by selling gold according to a prearranged schedule.

According to the World Gold Council, nearly 29,500 metric tons of gold is held in reserves by central banks around the world. The United States is the largest holder of gold with more than 8,100 metric tons, representing around 76.5 percent of currency reserves. Germany holds approximately 3,400 metric tons. Western central banks generally have far greater gold holdings than Eastern ones. While China is chock-full of foreign currency reserves, its gold holdings are small—just 600 metric tons, or roughly 0.9 percent of the country's total foreign currency reserves.

Baubles, Bangles, and Bling

Jewelry is far and away the biggest demand driver for gold. And lately, getting decked out in baubles and bangles will cost you plenty. With the price of gold hitting fresh highs, bling-lovers are now on a budget. At the height of the global economic crisis in November and December of 2008, luxury jeweler Tiffany & Co. reported that sales in their American stores plunged 35 percent. But when lovers start shunning gold, investors cozy up to coins and bars.

Gold is viewed as a status symbol throughout Asia, but nowhere is it more prized than in India, where gold jewelry is the centerpiece of the gift-giving festival season. Mistrust of government runs high in India, and since gold can't be debased and can be converted to cash in a hurry, it's seen as a solid investment. Savers wary of mutual funds can conveniently buy gold at one of India's post offices, which sell 24-carat coins in weights as small as 0.5 grams. Lately, India has been experiencing a gold rush, as rapid expansion has raised the economic prospects for millions and increased the demand for gold. From 2000 to 2007, Indian demand accounted for one ounce out of every nine sold worldwide. So significant is India to the gold market that gold prices experience strong seasonal trends—rising in the late summer and fall as the festival season begins.

Billion Dollar Baby

As the printing presses on Pennsylvania Avenue and at central banks around the world begin to hum, physical gold has become a hot commodity among investors. Having once been the linchpin of the global monetary system, gold is still seen by many as a solid hedge against inflation. And dealers of gold coins and bars are reporting a surge in interest from those worried by paltry returns on savings accounts and recent stock market volatility. Bullion dealers in London reported particularly strong interest after Lehman Brothers collapsed in September 2008. Gold coins from South Africa, known as Krugerrands, have also been switching hands frequently as of late, often at hefty premiums to the spot price of gold (about 13 percent above gold's prevailing market price). The price of a gold coin varies widely, depending not only on the value of gold at the time, but also on its scarcity, value, and manufacturing cost.

Gold coins have been popular, but gold bars, whose premiums are closer to 5 percent, offer better value. Of course, getting that price means buying in bulk, and once the cost of storage and insurance are factored in, holding physical bars or coins as an investment makes no sense. However, for many the peace of mind that comes with holding physical gold is worth the cost. They believe that if the world as we know it comes to an end, physical gold will continue to hold its value.

The big thing in gold investing these days is the explosive growth in exchange traded funds (ETFs) that track the price of gold. An ETF investment offers direct exposure to a financial interest in stockpiles of physical gold at a fraction of the cost of holding your own stash. And with management expense ratios of less than 1 percent, it's a wonder anyone would consider owning physical gold in any other form. It's a benefit that has not gone unnoticed. By the beginning of 2010, the world's major gold-linked ETFs held a staggering 1,821 metric tons of gold, worth more than $58.5 billion.

~

Gold bars are cheaper to own than coins, but both forms will incur storage and insurance fees. An investment in an ETF offers direct exposure to a financial interest in stockpiles of physical gold at a fraction of the cost of holding your own stash.

The largest gold ETF is the SPDR Gold Shares (GLD—NYSE), which accounts for around 65 percent of the total gold ETF market by market capitalization. Capital flows into GLD have been so strong that the fund now boasts a higher market value than Barrick Gold Corp. (ABX—NYSE), the world's biggest gold mining company.

My Two Cents

An investment in gold would seem to be a sure thing, with plenty of upside and not much downside. Perhaps it's a case of familiarity breeding contempt, but I can't help wondering if gold will really rally as high as some of the other precious metals. In the investment funds that I manage, I tend to look to gold as a trade, rather than as an investment. If the dollar index futures appear to be weakening (declining DXY—ICE), then I buy all the well-chosen gold equities that I can squeeze into my portfolios, but if the inflation picture is muted and the dollar isn't dropping, I can usually get more bang for my buck elsewhere.

For investors looking for direct exposure to the metal, I favor buying shares in the GLD rather than filling a safety deposit box chock full of gold bars. The GLD will give you all of the upside of owning the metal directly, without the headaches and high costs. By the end of 2009, two big hitters on Wall Street—John Paulson and George Soros—made news when it was revealed that GLD was amongst their top investment holdings. For my money, that's a pretty solid endorsement for owning a gold ETF.

The Family Silver

Silver, gold's slightly shy sister, is also in hot demand when gold's fortunes are rising. Like gold, silver acts as money and as a store of value. Gold and silver prices have historically moved in lockstep, zigging and zagging together, but lately, that correlation has broken down— gold has soared, while silver has slumped. From 1999 to 2009, the two metals moved together only 51 percent of the time. During 2009, the price ratio between the two averaged about 70:1—a huge increase from the 200-year average of 37:1. And that's got many investors excited about the possibility of a sharp upward correction in the price of silver.

Figure 5.1 Gold and Silver—Still Joined at the Hip?

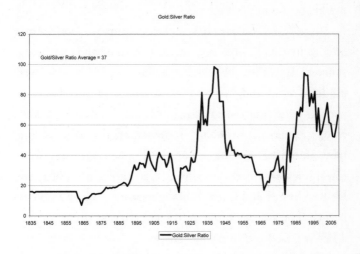

During 2009, the price ratio between gold and silver has averaged about 70:1—a huge increase from the 200-year average of 37:1.

If the price ratio between the two metals were to revert back to its historical average, then silver prices would outperform gold by more than 2:1. In fact, the physical ratio of silver to gold in the earth's crust is 16:1, so silver may be relatively cheap. During the inflationary 1970s, the ratio between gold and silver prices was at exactly 16:1—mirroring the proportions in which the two metals occur in nature.

Like gold, silver has been prized for its beauty and valued as a precious metal for thousands of years. Ancient Egyptians believed that the skin of the gods was made of gold and their bones of silver. It has also been used as a currency, most notably by the United Kingdom, whose pound (£) originally represented the value of one troy pound of sterling silver. In France, the very word for money is *argent*, or silver. Up until the 1800s, the United States and Great Britain were on a silver standard before they switched to a gold standard and then, later, to a paper-based monetary system.

Silver has similar investment attributes to gold. It can be used as a hedge against financial ruin, or, for a fat premium to value, you can buy coins or bars and store them somewhere safe. Silverware adorns many dining room tables, and silver is a mainstay of the jewelry industry. Investors can buy the stocks of silver-producing companies or invest in silver ETFs. Silver is used 50 percent of the time as an industrial metal. Gold, on the other hand, is used as an industrial metal a scant 11 percent of the time.

Silver Lining

Silver demand sits on a solid fundamental footing, while gold demand is just too dependent on fickle investment flows and flights of fancy from jewelry buyers in the Middle East and Asia. But when gold prices turn higher and industrial demand recovers, silver investors will be laughing all the way to the bank.

The Anatolia region in Turkey was the first area to be mined primarily for silver. Following Europe's discovery of the New World, production shifted to Bolivia, Peru, and Mexico, and then later to the United States. Today, 70 percent of all silver is mined along with other metals, typically lead, zinc, and copper. Globally, annual silver production is more than 600 million ounces (1.7 kilograms) and growing, while gold production is around 80 million ounces (2.3 kilograms) and declining.

The Silver Screen

Silver was once used in photography and in a host of industrial applications. Now, the use of silver in photography has tumbled as digital cameras have become all the rage. However, investment (ETFs) and other industrial uses have more than offset the 30 percent of mine supply that photography historically soaked up. With the highest conductivity of all the metals, silver is used in electrical contacts and conductors, and is finding new uses in LCD and plasma screens as well as in silver-zinc batteries. It also serves as a catalyst for chemical reactions and as an industrial coating on mirrors and solar panels.

Silver also has a number of medical uses. The father of medicine, Hippocrates, wrote that silver had beneficial healing and disease-fighting properties. The Phoenicians used to store water and wine in silver bottles to prevent spoiling. Today, silver is known to reduce or eliminate the risks associated with Legionnaires' disease and other superbugs resistant to traditional antibiotics.

Despite rising prices, industrial demand for silver increased each and every year from 2001 to 2007. Widespread computerization and the growing use of mobile phones are all positive trends that will help underpin future silver demand. Investment demand is also on the upswing. Coin sales and the issuance of new silver-linked ETFs have been doing a brisk business based on investors reasoning that, with increasing demand and a price ratio between gold and silver that's way out of whack from historical norms, silver prices could be ready to move solidly higher.

Platinum: The New Gold

Gold helped put South Africa's economy on the world map over a century ago, but today, with its reserves dwindling and its mines going ever deeper, South Africa's gold production is down while its costs are up. And that has many mining companies switching to the new "it" metal: platinum. In 2006, sales of platinum group metals (PGMs)—platinum, palladium, and rhodium—mined in South Africa outstripped gold by 2:1 and accounted for 15 percent of merchandise exports. And no wonder—South Africa has enormous platinum reserves that make up around 80 percent of the world total. This big reserve base, combined with the country's impressive mining expertise, have turned South Africa into the world's biggest platinum producer, with annual production of more than 5.1 million ounces. The country supplies 76 percent of the roughly six million ounces of platinum the world consumes. In fact, South Africa now has about as many mining companies drilling for platinum as for gold, which was good news for shareholders in 2006, when platinum group metals sales were twice those of gold.

Platinum mining is bringing good fortune to mining companies in South Africa, but, unfortunately, that hasn't been the case for foreign firms operating in Zimbabwe—home of the second-largest platinum reserves in the world.

Zimbabwe began mining platinum as recently as 1994, and by 2005 it was already the fourth-largest producer of the metal. In March 2006, as platinum prices started moving higher, Zimbabwe's minister of mines announced that 51 percent of the country's foreign mining share-holdings were to be transferred to the government—half without compensation.

Love in the Fast Lane

Couples show their undying love by exchanging rings, many made of platinum. The metal may be popular for wedding rings, but jewelry accounts for just 21 percent of its overall demand, down from 45 percent in 1999. China is to platinum what India is to gold: the largest single market for jewelry made from the metal.

But the big driver of platinum demand today isn't lovers, it's cars. The automotive industry sucks up more platinum than any other single industry, where it's used in catalytic converters to reduce exhaust emissions.

───────── ∽ ─────────

South Africa mines almost 76 percent of the world's platinum, which is turned into jewelry and catalytic converters for cars.

Driving an increased demand for catalytic converters and platinum are stricter environmental standards, which have helped boost the amount of platinum used per converter. More drivers in Asia and Europe and tougher environmental standards have been a winning combination for platinum investors. The auto industry accounts for a hefty 48 percent of overall demand for the metal. As platinum prices surged in the mid-1990s, North American car companies began redesigning their gasoline engines to use cheaper catalysts, such as palladium and rhodium. That left Europe, with 53 percent of the light diesel vehicle market, and Asia, with 30 percent of the overall market, as the big drivers of industrial demand for platinum. America, with only 4 percent of the global light diesel vehicle market, just isn't that important when it comes to boosting platinum demand.

In hybrid cars, the use of platinum group metals is even higher than in conventional cars. Automobiles such as the Toyota Prius, which can run on both electricity and gasoline, have engines that operate at cooler temperatures than regular cars, requiring more PGM loadings. And since platinum is a better catalyst than palladium, strong hybrid sales are good news for platinum investors.

Metal Meddling?

Investment interest in platinum is growing, yet the launch of ETFs linked to platinum has raised concerns that speculative activity in such a small market may drive prices higher. Platinum and gold prices have historically moved in lockstep, but platinum has seen higher highs and lower lows. In July 2008, platinum prices were more than $1,900 per ounce, but by October of the same year, prices tumbled to around $760 per ounce. Slumping industrial production, big investment flows in a tight market, and concern over labor unrest and electricity disruptions in South Africa all helped make platinum a volatile investment in 2008.

Hammer and Sickle

Platinum's lighter, less expensive cousin is palladium—a metal used in cars, jewelry, and electrical applications. Diesel, which requires platinum catalytic converters, is the predominant automotive fuel in Europe. However, 82 percent of the world's cars run on gasoline, which can use palladium, a cheaper metal. As with platinum, the car industry represents around 48 percent of total demand for palladium, while jewelry and electrical uses account for around 15 percent each. Automotive demand for palladium began picking up around 1994, as technological advancements in catalytic converters were made and U.S. relations with Russia improved. South Africa dominates the platinum supply, but Russia, which contributes 52 percent of the global mine supply, is the hammer in palladium production.

Globally, Russian mining giant Norilsk Nickel is the largest single producer of nickel and palladium. With production of close to three million ounces of palladium annually, the company supplies around 45 percent of the roughly 6.5-million-ounce global market. The company's largest operations are centered in the Norilsk-Talnakh region of northern Russia, an area known to have the single largest nickel-copper-palladium deposits in the world. Since acquiring Stillwater Mining Company in 2003, the only U.S. producer of palladium, Norilsk Nickel has become a global behemoth. In 2007, it extended its global reach even further, acquiring assets in Finland, South Africa, Botswana, and Australia.

Bling Fling

As the U.S. and Europe warm up the printing presses to help monetize the staggering debts they've rung up over the last 25 years, investors will flock to the traditional safe havens of gold and silver. And once the global economy gets back onto solid footing and industrial production accelerates, the prospect for an investment in precious metals becomes even more promising.

Gold producers have historically offered leverage to rising gold prices, making them a solid way to play the gold market. Once they get underground and look around, most major producers have a pretty good track record when it comes to discovering more gold. Barrick Gold Corporation (ABX—NYSE), the largest gold company in the world with 27 mines and operations on five continents, is a true mining multinational. Since silver is usually mined along with other metals, finding a pure-play silver producer can be something of a challenge. Of the 20 largest silver-producing companies in the world, only five (Fresnillo Plc, Pan American Silver, Polymetal, Coeur d'Alene Mines, and Hecla Mining) are primary silver producers. One way to play the silver story is through silver streaming companies such as Silver Wheaton (SLW—S&P/TSX) or Franco-Nevada (FNV—S&P/TSX). Silver streaming companies purchase silver production for many years into the future from diversified mining companies focused on recovering metals other than silver. The benefit of investing in these companies is that they offer direct leverage to rising silver prices with no operational risks or ongoing capital expenditure requirements.

Those looking to invest in the niche markets of platinum and palladium should consider investing in an exchange traded fund because finding a pure-play North American palladium producer is next to impossible and there isn't a wide range of choice for platinum producers. The three largest platinum producers in the world are Anglo Platinum (AMS–JO) and Impala Platinum Holdings Limited (IMP–JO), both of which trade on the Johannesburg stock exchange, and Lonmin (LMI–LSE), which trades in London. ETF Securities offers the largest market capitalization physically backed platinum (PHPT–LSE) and palladium (PHPD–LSE) exchange traded funds.

Declining grades, surging investor demand, and recovering global industrial production have set the stage for a pickup in the precious metals market. Propelled by a strong tailwind of too many dollars, yen, and euros chasing after a limited supply of gold, silver, and PGMs, precious metal investors will soon be thanking their lucky stars for the ongoing financial follies coming out of Washington, Brussels, and London.

Hot Commodities

- Gold and other precious metals often outperform stocks, real estate, and bonds when banks are under stress, the U.S. dollar is weak, and inflation is running rampant.

- Gold last peaked in 1980 at $850 per ounce, the inflation-adjusted equivalent of $2,189 per ounce in 2009 dollars.

- Nearly 90 percent of known gold, with an approximate value of $4.5 trillion, has already been mined.

- The value of physical gold is dwarfed by the value of paper-based financial assets, such as the $800 trillion notional value of the world's derivative securities.

- An investment in an ETF offers direct exposure to a financial interest in stockpiles of physical gold at a fraction of the cost of holding your own stash.

- Silver does best when gold is performing well and industrial activity is high.

- During 2009, the price ratio between gold and silver has averaged about 70:1—a huge increase from the 200-year average of 32:1.

- South Africa mines almost 76 percent of the world's platinum, most of which is turned into jewelry and catalytic converters for cars.

- Russia is the largest producer of palladium, a metal with similar end-markets to platinum.

Chapter Six

Digging It

~

Making Metals and Mines Work for You

IF YOU WANT TO SWILL VODKA AND EAT CAVIAR like a Russian oligarch, nothing will get you there faster than a well-timed investment in industrial metals. Whenever cars, washing machines, and fridges are selling like hotcakes you can be certain that metals and the mining companies that produce them will be moving higher. Research has shown that once global industrial production (IP) begins to accelerate, commodity prices for hot rolled steel, copper, aluminum, and zinc are the first to move. And as the world economy begins to grow again, the metals used in cars, toys, and kitchen appliances will be in strong demand, which will send prices—and the fortunes of investors—sharply higher.

Commodity prices for hot rolled steel, copper, aluminum, and zinc are the first to move when global industrial production begins to accelerate.

Kerplunk

When the global economy fell out of bed in the fall of 2008, factories slammed their doors shut and industrial production careened off a cliff. Detroit's drastically reduced car manufacturing prowess took an even bigger blow when General Motors, once the largest carmaker in the world, declared bankruptcy. Demand for cars, iPods, flat-screen TVs, and washing machines tumbled across the globe, and manufacturers jammed on the brakes, shutting down factories and laying off workers.

As factories closed, industrial metals prices dropped like a stone, wiping out fortunes and closing down mines. Copper, a metal used in both industrial and electronic applications, saw its price peak in April 2008 at $3.96 per pound. By the end of 2008, however, copper prices had slumped by more than two-thirds while nickel, a metal most often used in the production of stainless steel, fell more than 72 percent from peak to trough. Metals traders, terrified of a world that appeared to be hopelessly broken, decided to sell first and ask questions later.

Perhaps no one symbolized the highs and lows of the global metals business more than the notorious Russian oligarchs, a group of pirate capitalists who controlled some of Russia's most important resource industries. Yet even for this apparently bulletproof group, the downturn in the metals market has been ugly. Before the collapse, Oleg Deripaska was Russia's richest man, with a fortune of around $28 billion. The crown jewel of his empire was UC Rusal, the world's top aluminum producer. But excessive corporate and personal debt proved a deadly one-two combination for Deripaska. The crunch decimated his fortune, reducing it to just $3.5 billion and turning UC Rusal into a ward of the state.

Heavy Metals

Heavy metal bands came and went, but heavy metals are here to stay. The heavy metals, or "base metals" as they are often called, are the backbone of the world's industrial economy and are used in cars, buildings, and just about every consumer item you can think of.

Copper

The Statue of Liberty is made out of 81 metric tons of copper, one of the oldest known metals. Prized for its corrosion resistance as well as its electrical and heat conductivity, copper is used in a myriad of applications—everything from electrical wiring and copper pipes to brass musical instruments. Globally, construction and electronic applications account for 60 percent of copper demand.

As the go-to industrial metal, mining companies are always on the lookout for copper. But even for the mining giants of the world, finding economical deposits of copper to mine is no easy task. Typical ore, or mineral-bearing rock, contains as little as 0.5 to 2 percent copper, with an average grade of 1 percent. These days, Chile is doing the heavy lifting in the world of copper, producing 35 percent of the world's mine supply, but new areas such as Mongolia, Zambia, and the Democratic Republic of the Congo also look promising.

Aluminum

The foil wrap that you use to store your leftovers is made from aluminum—the most abundant of all metallic elements. One-third the weight of steel but equally strong, aluminum gets called upon for a wide range of construction and transportation applications—the average car, for instance, contains more than 250 pounds of aluminum. Of all the metals, aluminum is the second-best conductor of electricity, making it ideal for use in power transmission lines. Finding and mining bauxite, the ore that contains aluminum oxide (alumina), is relatively easy. But converting bauxite into aluminum requires a smelter and lots of electrical power to run the operations, which is why access to cheap power, rather than proximity to bauxite deposits, is the key factor in aluminum production.

Nickel

If you ever decide it's time to throw everything out, including the kitchen sink, you might want to think again. Kitchen sinks, and a whole host of other consumer and industrial products, contain nickel, a metal that can be combined with steel to form stainless steel. The fortunes of nickel are thus closely tied to the demand for stainless steel, which is used in the production of cars, aircraft, and consumer products. Nickel is relatively abundant, yet just three countries—Russia, Canada, and Australia—are responsible for almost half of its global supply.

Zinc

The red-headed stepchild of the large-scale mining business is zinc, a metal commonly used in the automotive and construction industries. Zinc is often coated onto steel or iron in a process known as galvanizing, which increases corrosion resistance. Nearly half of all zinc demand comes from the construction industry, which uses galvanized steel in floor systems, roofing materials, and ductwork for heating and air conditioning.

Zinc is an extremely useful industrial metal that has the unusual disadvantage of being reasonably abundant. China has both enormous zinc reserves and thousands of artisanal miners willing to grab their picks and shovels and head underground, Seven Dwarfs style, when prices are high. Zinc ore's relatively high grade (typically 5 to 15 percent), ease of recycling, and the intense competition among its many small-scale artisanal miners all conspire to make it the least favored of major metals to mine. Both BHP Billiton and Rio Tinto, two of the biggest mining companies in the world, have been loath to get into zinc mining, even though the barriers to entry aren't all that formidable.

The world's top 10 zinc mining companies churn out about 40 percent of total mine production, but just three countries—Australia, China, and Peru—hold about half of the world's known zinc reserves. The two biggest players in the world of zinc mining are Anglo/Swiss giant Xstrata PLC (XTA—LSE) and Canadian mining major Teck Resources Ltd. (TCK—NYSE).

Lead

Despite being a soft metal, lead is surprisingly heavy. It's useful for ballast in the keel of sailboats, but most of the time (81 percent) it's used in batteries. In China, a popular form of transportation these days is a battery-powered motor scooter known as the e-bike. With more than 80 million currently in circulation and an additional 20 million a year rolling off the assembly line, e-bike manufacturing alone will ensure that lead demand stays strong.

Tin

The odds of discovering tin are very low indeed. As the 49th most abundant element in the earth's crust, tin is relatively rare. Today, people often incorrectly attribute the term tin to anything shiny; tin foil and tin cans are prime examples of this mistake. Most of these products are made from aluminum, however, not tin. Tin's corrosion resistance makes it ideal for combining with steel, but its most common application is as a solder for joining together pipes or electric circuits.

Metal Fatigue

Mines were closed and exploration activity ground to a halt during the global financial crisis of 2008–2009. As metals prices tumbled and financing evaporated, lots of junior mining companies went belly-up as global mine supply, already struggling before the collapse, crash-landed.

Once the world's factories get back up to full steam, metals and mines will once again be in high demand. That being said, getting a mine built and into production is no small feat. Mining analyst Larry Smith of Scotia Capital has estimated that an average copper mine can cost as much as $12,000 to $15,000 per metric ton of annual capacity to build. This means that a mine capable of producing 200,000 metric tons of copper a year could cost upwards of $2.4 billion to put into operation—which is hardly bush-league. Then there's the long wait time, sometimes more than a couple of years, for environmental assessments and permitting. What's more, if the mining market is hot, lead times for critical mining or milling equipment can take anywhere from 12 to 36 months from the time of order until the stuff actually hits the site. The bottom line is that it takes at least five years and *big* bucks to get a mine into full production once economically viable quantities of copper, nickel, or zinc have been discovered.

---~---

It takes big bucks and at least five years to get a mine up and running and into full production once economically viable quantities of copper, nickel, or zinc have been discovered.

Once a mine is up and running, miners first have to blast and drill through copious quantities of rock before any metal can be recovered and this is only getting more difficult over time. The percentage of metal in ore, or the "grade," is declining in the traditional mining regions of the world, and lower-grade mines mean that more ore needs to be processed through the mill to get the equivalent production of a higher-grade mine. Western mining companies are often faced with a difficult choice: either they mine lower-grade, less efficient deposits in mining-friendly jurisdictions or they pursue higher-grade projects in politically unstable regions of the world.

Out of Africa

One country that holds tremendous promise for our copper-hungry world is the Democratic Republic of the Congo (DRC), which is blessed with immense mineral wealth—it is the world's largest producer of cobalt and a significant supplier of industrial diamonds—but, unfortunately, not a whole lot else. For most of its 50-year existence, the country formerly known as Zaire has been in a constant state of crisis, plagued by civil war and decades of authoritarian rule under strongman Mobutu Sese Seko. In 1994, the country's annual rate of inflation hit a staggering 10,000 percent. In 1997, the DRC exported just $2.6 billion worth of goods—a paltry sum for a country of 60 million people. It should come as no surprise that over the last several years the World Bank has consistently ranked the DRC as the worst place in the world to conduct business.

Yet despite this abysmal record, mining companies are setting up shop in the DRC in the hope of capitalizing on copper deposits in the country's southern Katanga province. And the Congolese, for their part, are so poor they have little choice but to welcome whatever foreign capital they can get. In 2007, China's Export-Import Bank, through which the country disburses its foreign aid, pledged $2 billion toward mine refurbishment programs and another $6.5 billion for general infrastructure developments within the DRC. To get access to the country's resources, the Chinese companies have had to do more than simply put up cash—they've had to hire a raft of locals and also take on Gécamines, the state-owned mining company, as a partner.

The Chinese aren't the only ones trying to develop mining projects in the DRC. American mining conglomerate Freeport-McMoRan (FCX—NYSE) has been trying to get the Tenke Fungurume copper mine in Katanga province into production for more than a decade. Although various prospective investors have dropped out of Freeport's mining consortium over the decade out of concern for the DRC's instability, the project is now finally moving ahead with financial backing from the European Investment Bank, America's Overseas Private Investment Corporation, and the African Development Bank. Adding to investors' anxiety, the DRC's government is conducting an opaque, lengthy review of all mining contracts signed during the country's civil war. Canadian copper mining company First Quantum Minerals Ltd. (FM—S&P/TSX) has been battling with the DRC over the status of their Kolwezi copper-cobalt project for years. In August 2009, First Quantum received a letter from the DRC's prime minister effectively demanding the return of the mining permit for the project. The DRC is an extreme example, but expropriation, civil unrest, and a near-absence of private property rights are unfortunately all too common in many parts of the world where global mining companies operate.

The 800-Pound Gorilla

The 800-pound gorilla of metals demand is China, whose appetite for commodities of all stripes is voracious. Over the last 30 years, more than 621 million Chinese have moved out of extreme poverty to join the ranks of the global consumer. And like consumers everywhere, the Chinese have an almost insatiable desire for more stuff—the difference being that when more than a billion people are suddenly vying for a slice of the middle-class lifestyle, they will *not* be denied.

China is the 800-pound gorilla of commodity consumption, accounting for nearly 100 percent of global demand growth for copper during the 2007 bull market in industrial metals.

The rapid urbanization of China is spurring a bull market in commodities, and industrial metals in particular, as millions of people there, and in the developing world generally, demand consumer goods such as appliances and automobiles. And as the world's factory, China is all too happy to oblige. According to Barclays Capital, China accounted for almost 100 percent of the global demand growth for copper during the 2007 bull market in industrial metals.

Figure 6.1 China Consumes Commodities!
(Percentage of Total Global Demand, 2008)

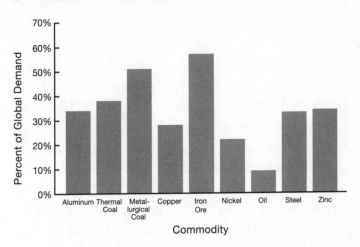

With roughly a quarter of the world's population, global demand growth in industrial metals has been driven almost entirely by China's enormous economic expansion. China is number one in alumina production (from which aluminum is made), which increased by almost 400 percent from 2000 to 2007 despite the fact that the country has only 2.8 percent of the world's bauxite reserves. While copper-smelting capacity in the United States shrank by 60 percent over the last decade, in China it *doubled*, making the country the largest producer of refined copper. China is the largest consumer of zinc (it tripled its consumption of the metal during the past decade) and stainless steel—an important driver of nickel demand.

London Calling

If you're looking for the Mecca of metals trading, then London is it. The activity level on the London Metals Exchange (LME) simply dwarfs that of the COMEX, its nearest competitor market. The most actively traded metal contracts on the fast and furious LME are those of aluminum, copper, zinc, and nickel. Unlike other futures markets where one-month contracts are the norm, the actively traded metals futures on the LME are rolling three-month contracts—a reflection of the average time that a metal spends in process inventory; that is, the time it takes to move from mine mouth to smelter, including the time it spends at sea.

———————————— ∿ ————————————

Unlike other futures markets, the actively traded metal futures on the LME are rolling three-month contracts. This reflects the average time that metal is in process inventory—moving from mine mouth to smelter, including the time at sea.

The LME also differs from the NYMEX in that it functions as a warehouse for finished products. It does this by licensing a series of storage facilities next to major manufacturing hubs throughout the world. The inventory levels within these LME facilities form an important, widely followed barometer of the health of the industrial metals market. If inventory levels are high, it's generally safe to conclude that demand for metals is weak. However, if the exchange is experiencing a rising level of cancelled warrants, this indicates that metals demand is firming up. Why? Because LME inventories are reduced when metal moves out of storage and into factories, and a warrant, or certificate of title, must be presented to the exchange for cancellation *before* the metal can be booked for shipment.

Springing a Leak?

Five hundred and forty-six yards (500 meters) below the earth's surface lies the highest-grade uranium ore body in the world: Cameco Corporation's McArthur River property. Ventilation, underground flooding, and mine safety are all important considerations in underground mining, but with uranium they're crucial. During the summer of 2009, I visited the McArthur River mine and was blown away by the ingeniousness of Cameco's (CCO—S&P/TSX) mining engineers in overcoming tremendous technical challenges to produce uranium from McArthur River.

Uranium ore bodies are often found in porous rocks such as sandstone. If underground streams are present, however, water incursion in the mine can quickly become a serious problem, as was the case at McArthur River. To solve it, Cameco's engineers devised a nifty solution. Before beginning large-scale mining, they first cleared horizontal tunnels, or "drifts," running adjacent to the uranium ore. Miners then drilled a series of holes through the middle of the ore body and down to another drift that has been cleared more than 109 yards (100 meters) below. The holes were filled with metal piping, through which a brine solution, chilled to minus 22 degrees Fahrenheit (minus 30 degree Celsius), was pumped. Seven months later, a section of the mine has turned into a giant ice cube that can be safely mined without the worry of underground flooding.

Nuke Reboot

As environmentalists fret over America's dependence on coal-fired power generation, nuclear power is enjoying a renaissance. Not only is nuclear power one of the cleanest forms of electrical generation around, but in an era of runaway commodity prices, nuclear plants are cheap to operate. Uranium, the fuel used by nuclear power plants, represents about 25 percent of the total operating cost—a

far cry from the nearly 91 percent that natural gas represents to a gas-fired plant.

─────────────── ∼ ───────────────

**Nuclear power is one of the most
environmentally friendly ways to generate electric
power. Fuel costs for nuclear power plants are
extremely low when compared with oil, coal, or
natural gas-fired alternatives for generating power.**

─────────────────────────────────

Today, worries about core meltdowns seem a thing of
the past, and younger generations are embracing, rather
than fearing, nuclear power. Approximately 17 percent
of the world's electricity is generated by nuclear power
at some 440 power plants, and France, which generates
around 78 percent of its power from nukes, is at the
industry's forefront. What's more, with environmental
concerns starting to become a major issue in China, uranium and nuclear power are likely to experience strong
demand for years to come.

Nine companies worldwide are responsible for nearly
90 percent of global uranium production. France may
be a leader in nuclear power generation, but just two
countries—Australia and Canada—produce almost half
of the world's total mined uranium; Canada's Cameco
(which supplies 16 percent of world demand) is the

largest producer. Total mined uranium production is 110 million pounds a year, or 64 percent of electric utilities' fuel requirements. The remaining third comes from decommissioned Russian nuclear weapons and other forms of secondary supply from around the world.

Metal Mania

As the world's steel mills, factories, and manufacturing facilities gear up, metals prices are sure to move higher. When the global financial crisis of 2008–2009 hit, miners everywhere dropped their picks and shovels and headed for the hills as companies with development projects in the works went into care-and-maintenance mode to wait out the economic storm. Given that the average mine takes a rock-bottom minimum of five years to bring into production, supply will indisputably lag demand as the global economy begins to expand, and this will mean sharply higher metals prices for a long, long time to come.

Hot Commodities

- Commodity prices for hot rolled steel, copper, aluminum, and zinc are the first to move when global industrial production begins to accelerate.

- It takes at least five years and big bucks to get a mine up and running and into full production once economically viable quantities of copper, nickel, or zinc have been discovered.

- China is the 800-pound gorilla of commodity consumption, accounting for nearly 100 percent of global demand growth for copper during the 2007 bull market in industrial metals.

- Near-month LME futures contracts are traded on a rolling three-month basis.

- Metals traders carefully follow the inventory levels of metals on the LME, as they serve as an important barometer of industrial demand.

- Nuclear power is experiencing a renaissance, and uranium prices will likely move higher as concerns over the environment take center stage globally.

Chapter Seven

Betting the Farm

~

Bingeing on Food Inflation

OVER ONE BILLION PEOPLE WORLDWIDE go to bed hungry every night. And that figure is likely to climb as changing diets, rapid urbanization, and global population growth combine to raise food prices dramatically. At the United Nations' first World Food Conference in 1974, American Secretary of State Henry Kissinger pledged to end child hunger within the next 10 years. More than 35 years later, however, global hunger is still a problem, one that will likely get worse. According to the United Nations Food and Agriculture Organization (FAO), between now and 2050 the world's population will increase by more than a third, the demand for agricultural products will rise by more than 70 percent, and the global demand for meat will double. Food prices must rise to encourage farmers to grow more food to feed a hungry planet—a circumstance that will ensure that millions more of the world's poor will go to bed hungry in the future.

Food Fight

Rising food prices are like a silent tsunami, shaking governments and stoking riots in their wake. In the West, where food expenditures account for less than 15 percent of personal income, rising prices are an annoyance, but in the developing world, where this figure can rise as high as 80 percent, they're a catastrophe. In 2007, wheat prices shot up 77 percent while the cost of rice, a staple in half the world's diets, rose 16 percent. In April 2008, World Bank President Bob Zoellick warned that 33 nations were at risk for social unrest because of rising food prices. During the same month, Prime Minister Jacques-Édouard Alexis of Haiti was forced from office as riots over the high cost of beans, rice, and other food staples spread from the south of his country to the nation's capital. United Nations peacekeepers trying to restore calm were pressed into action, shooting tear gas canisters and rubber bullets at thousands of rioters who had paralyzed the capital. In March 2008, Egypt's President Hosni Mubarak ordered his army to start baking bread after skyrocketing wheat prices led to social unrest. According to the World Bank's Zoellick, "For countries where food comprises from half to three-quarters of consumption, there is no margin for survival." Faced with the stark choice of rioting or starving, many of the world's poor have been forced into the streets.

In the West, food expenditures account for less than 15 percent of personal income, but in the developing world, this figure can rise as high as 80 percent.

About one billion people live on only a dollar a day—the benchmark for extreme poverty. For these people, many of whom have been forced to pull their children from school and to cut back on vegetables so they can still afford to eat rice, malnutrition and misery are the unpleasant repercussions of rising food prices. If food inflation persists, a further 100 million people may be pushed into extreme poverty.

About one billion people live on only a dollar a day—the benchmark for extreme poverty.

The recent price surge marked an end to a nearly 30-year period of cheap, stable food prices. Throughout much of the world, farming is highly subsidized and regulated through a byzantine system of quotas and other restrictions. For most governments, food security ranks right up there with energy security, and the viability of a nation's domestic agricultural industry is often vigorously protected through an aggressive array of tariffs. And as with any highly protected industry, inefficiency is often the order of the day. Because local governments, rather than the global marketplace, supply the pricing signals, many Western farmers have actually found themselves in the bizarre situation of being paid *not* to farm.

During the Green Revolution of the 1960s, advances in seed varieties and the use of pesticides helped increase crop yields by between 3 to 6 percent per year. As word of these new higher-yield seed types spread, adoption by farmers was swift. By the 1970s, some 40 percent of farmers in the developing world were using Green Revolution seeds and global food supplies were rapidly expanding.

From 1954 to 1963, much of America's surplus grain was exported to poor countries under the USAID program, peaking at 17 million metric tons in the 1965–1966 growing season. Today, America still dominates the international food aid system, providing more than half of all global food assistance.

Over the last 25 years, however, investments in farming have declined steadily. Between 1980 and 2006, Western agricultural aid decreased by 75 percent, while developing countries managed to invest only 5 percent of their government revenues in farming. Political instability, food inflation, and governmental neglect have further exacerbated the differences between the agricultural haves and have-nots. Making matters worse, the rate of crop yield growth has flatlined in poor countries and slowed to between 1 and 2 percent in rich countries. Continued food inflation seems the likeliest outcome of this combination of dwindling surpluses in the West and struggling supply throughout the developing world. Joachim von Braun, the head of the International Food Policy Research Institute in Washington, D.C., is concerned that the world may be in for a nasty food fight, warning in the April 19, 2008, edition of *The Economist* that "World agriculture has entered a new, unsustainable and politically risky period."

Land Grab

During the global food scare of 2007–2008, as food prices experienced their sharpest rise in 30 years, riots swept through three dozen countries. Many large food-producing nations hoarded key crops and banned their export. During 2008, Vietnam and Thailand, the world's biggest exporters of rice, wrought havoc in the Philippines—the world's biggest importer of rice— by banning the grain's export. For countries like the Philippines, the lesson from the most recent price spike was obvious: world markets could no longer be trusted to supply their needs.

Increasingly, countries are moving toward greater food self-sufficiency in an attempt to curb their reliance on the international market. The Philippines, for example, has a goal of growing 98 percent of the rice it needs by 2010. In 2008, Indonesian President Susilo Bambang Yudhoyono announced big increases in farm subsidies as a first move toward food self-sufficiency. Senegal, which imports more than 80 percent of its rice and was rocked by food riots in 2008, has responded to the crisis with a government blueprint for agricultural self-sufficiency in staple goods called the "Great Offensive for Food and Abundance." Elsewhere, Honduras, Malaysia, Colombia, and China are all currently pursuing similar goals.

In early 2009, Saudi Arabia received its first shipment of rice from Ethiopia—the result of a $100 million investment program aimed at raising rice, wheat, and barley on foreign soil. With mistrust of the international grain markets running high, Saudi Arabia's move was part of a larger trend—wealthy grain-importing countries outsourcing grain production to poorer, land-rich countries in need of investment. In recent years, China, Kuwait, and South Korea have all opted to grow food on land they control abroad rather than rely on imports, and already some of the best farmland in poor countries has been spoken for by foreign interests. By the end of 2009, nearly 50 million acres (20 hectares) of prime farmland was sold or under long-term lease.

———————— ∼ ————————

Already some of the best farmland in poor countries has been spoken for by foreign interests. By the end of 2009, nearly 50 million acres (20 hectares) of prime farmland was sold or under long-term lease in what amounts to a massive land grab.

Going Green?

High oil prices and pressure from environmentalists have forced lawmakers around the world to pass legislation mandating the use of biofuels. While the U.S. consumes about 21 million barrels of oil a day, it produces just 5.2 million—it imports the balance. In 2007, President Bush signed into law the *Energy Independence and Security Act* with the goal of weaning the U.S. off its dependence on foreign oil through the promotion of alternative fuels and the mandating of better vehicle fuel economy. The law stipulates that 36 billion gallons of biofuels—or fuel from food—must be added to gasoline by 2022. In America, the biofuel of choice is ethanol, a type of grain alcohol made from corn. When blended with gasoline, ethanol increases the octane level of the fuel and reduces the carbon monoxide emissions that cars produce.

But in spite of ethanol's apparent benefits as an eco-friendly fuel, the debate over its use rages on and serious doubts about its usefulness persist. In one study, David Pimentel, a professor of Ecology and Agriculture at Cornell University, found that it took 29 percent more energy to convert corn into ethanol than the fuel actually produced. Others have suggested that if every bushel of wheat, rice, soybeans, and corn in the U.S. were used to produce ethanol, it would still only cover about 4 percent of America's energy needs. In February 2008, the Associated Press cited the work of researchers affiliated with Princeton University who found that, due to expected land-use changes, the widespread use of corn-based ethanol could result in *twice* the greenhouse gas emissions of the gasoline it would replace.

Politicians concerned with going green have embraced biofuels as a potential answer to our addiction to fossil fuels. But by mandating a sixfold increase in the use of corn-based ethanol by 2022, they have boosted the demand for corn at precisely the same time that world demand for food is on the upswing. According to the International Monetary Fund (IMF), at least half of the rise in corn prices between 2005 and 2007 was attributable to corn ethanol production in the United States (since the U.S. produces about 42 percent of the world's corn, this should come as no surprise), and increases in biofuel production appear to be at least partly to blame for the single-year quadrupling of world corn prices that created a crisis for the poor from 2007 to 2008. In 2007, in response to the alarm over escalating prices, the United Nations' independent expert on the right to food called for a five-year moratorium on biofuel production from food crops.

This Little Piggy Went to Market

I enjoy a good steak every now and again, and as it turns out, my meat craving is shared globally. With rising incomes, a fundamental shift in eating patterns is occurring: as people become wealthier, they tend to eat more meat. In China, where half the world's pigs are raised and eaten, pork is the favorite meat-based protein, while in America, which produces and consumes the most poultry in the world, chicken reigns supreme. Brazil tips the scales as the world's largest producer of beef. While the world's appetite for meat continues to grow, nowhere is the demand as great as it is in the industrialized West. The average person in the developing world consumes just 62 pounds (28 kilograms) of meat per year, while Westerners consume a whopping 176 pounds (80 kilograms)—an almost threefold difference.

The developing world may lag behind the West in annual meat consumption per person, but the *overall* meat consumption rate is growing at twice the rate of population increases. Since meat is very grain- and water-intensive to produce, the dramatic increase in meat-based diets has profound agricultural implications. For example, it takes 4.4 pounds (two kilograms) of grain to produce 2.2 pounds (one kilogram) of chicken, and it can take as much as 22 pounds (10 kilograms) of grain and 180 gallons

(680 liters) of water to produce just 2.2 pounds (one kilogram) of beef. On the other hand, rice, which is the most water-intensive grain to produce, requires only one-tenth of the water needed to produce beef. In fact, the creation of a meat-rich diet is so resource intensive that, on average, it requires two to four times more land than is required for the creation of a vegetarian-based diet.

To meet this rising demand, millions of tons of grain—half the world's harvest—are currently being used as feed for livestock annually, but the FAO estimates that by 2030 a staggering one billion extra metric tons of cereal will be required to meet both human and animal needs.

— ∾ —

Half the world's grain harvest is fed to livestock, and the United Nations Food and Agricultural Organization (FAO) estimates that to meet human and animal needs an extra one billion metric tons of cereal will be required by 2030.

Nothing Runs Like a Deere

Three billion people globally make their living as farmers, about two billion of them on farms of less than 5 acres (two hectares). In Africa, small-scale farms represent around 80 percent of all agricultural output. In China, 92 percent of the farms are small subsistence farms. To feed a hungry planet, future focus will need to be on increasing the productivity of small-scale farms such as these.

In a September 2008 report, investment bank Credit Suisse cited farm commercialization—that is, any shift toward more sophisticated farming methods that helps produce greater, more consistent crops—as the single most important factor driving the next decade of growth in agriculture.

～

Investment bank Credit Suisse, in a September 2008 report, cited farm commercialization as the single most important factor driving the next decade of growth in agriculture.

Unfortunately, agricultural land is in short supply, and there are only so many national parks and forests that can be turned into farmers' fields. Over the coming years, this limitation, combined with growing demand from an expanding global population, will stress the food chain like never before. From 1961 to 2005, available agricultural land increased at just 0.2 percent per year; however, food production increased by 2 percent a year— a rate 10 times faster than the corresponding increases in arable land. The reasons for the massive improvement in productivity were simple: better agricultural practices in the form of superior seeds and fertilizers, coupled with improved pesticides and storage techniques.

—————————— ∼ ——————————

From 1961 to 2005, agricultural land increased at just 0.2 percent per year, however, food production increased by 2 percent a year—a rate 10 times faster than the corresponding increases in arable land.

During the bull market of 2007–2008, Western farmers responded to the run-up in world prices for grains by boosting their output. Harvests increased by 11 percent in rich nations, but sadly, in poor countries (India and China being the exceptions), grain output actually fell during that time period. Rising grain prices thus benefited farmers in the West, but penalized subsistence farmers who were unable to boost productivity and capitalize on the rising prices for grains.

Globally, levels of farm commercialization vary widely. During the 1930s, the family farm was the dominant feature of the American agricultural landscape. But by the 1960s, headlines warned of "faceless corporate behemoths" and "the end of the family farm" as large commercial enterprises bought up these small operations; the newspapers seemingly ignored the fact that the moves created economies of scale that brought lower food prices.

Brazil's and Argentina's moves toward greater farm commercialization began in the 1970s, and really picked up steam in the 1990s. In Eastern Europe and Russia, however, where the legacy of socialism has impeded the commercialization process, the story has been very different. In Russia, agricultural decision-making is still done locally rather than nationally, which has slowed the broad adoption of modern techniques.

China faces severe water pollution issues that will hamper its ability to commercialize its farms, but the country's interest in agricultural self-sufficiency and its powerful central planning apparatus mean that it could achieve large-scale farm commercialization within a decade. On the flip side, with close to 60 percent of China's total workforce active in farming, large-scale commercialization would mean massive dislocation and upheaval for millions of people.

As millions of small farms around the world get consolidated into larger commercial enterprises, massive investment in modern farm equipment will be needed to make them viable. Equipment manufacturers, such as giants Case New Holland (CNH—NYSE) and Deere and Company (DE—NYSE), should be prime beneficiaries of the global trend toward greater agricultural efficiency.

And that's only part of the good news story; once farmers select a tractor they tend to be extremely loyal to the brand—a loyalty that often extends for generations.

Money in Manure?

A major reason that North America leads the pack in terms of farm commercialization is its liberal use of commercial fertilizers. All fertilizers, including cow dung, provide critical nutrients, or plant food, that help spur crop growth and resist disease. Fertilized crops grow 30 to 50 percent faster than unfertilized crops, giving the commercial farms a huge leg up on the competition.

Fertilized crops grow 30 to 50 percent faster than unfertilized crops, giving the commercial farms a huge leg up on the competition.

In commercial farming, nothing is left to chance. Soil is analyzed, crop rotations are studied, and a precise regime of fertilization is worked out to ensure optimal growing conditions. There are a wide variety of commercial fertilizers available, all based on the three key plant nutrients from which they are derived—nitrogen, phosphate, and potassium—and all of which play a unique role in crop development.

Nitrogen-based fertilizers are made from natural gas and are the most prevalent, being used in 59 percent of all applications. Phosphate-based fertilizers are created by mixing crushed phosphate rock with water and sulfuric acid to produce phosphoric acid. Potassium-based fertilizers are created from potash (potassium chloride) and help to increase water retention and improve disease resistance in crops.

Access to cheap source deposits is the most important variable for fertilizer companies. While natural gas is pretty prevalent the world over, phosphate rock deposits are concentrated in Florida and Morocco, and only 12 countries are capable of supplying potash, the critical feedstock for making potassium-based fertilizers.

While Morocco is an interesting place to visit, Florida is closer, so recently I decided to check out some of Mosaic Company's (MOS—NYSE) operations in Florida to bone up on the phosphate business. To say that this was no Mickey Mouse operation is an understatement. Standing on the catwalk of an $80-million dragline while an operator swung the massive 350-foot-long (107-meter-long) boom towards the phosphate rock buried under a layer of clay and sand was quite the thrill. To turn the phosphate rock into a concentrate for further processing, a massive water cannon with enough force to cut a man in half is used to break apart the phosphate rock and turn it into a slurry (a mixture of water and phosphate). The slurry is then pumped eight miles to the plant for processing.

While you might think that the Florida landscape would look like one big gravel pit, land reclamation is a big part of the process of mining for phosphate rock. Old phosphate mines are transformed into wildlife preserves and nature habitats that leave no trace of the massive movement of rock and earth that came before. This seems like one smart way to be in the resource extraction business.

Dust Bunny

As the doors of the skip opened, I was surprised by how dusty the environment was. It was the summer of 2009, and I was visiting PotashCorp's flagship Lanigan mine in southern Saskatchewan. As one of the world's biggest potash mines, Lanigan is impressive. More than half a mile (one kilometer) below the earth's surface an enormous underground city unfolded before my eyes. We mounted modified half-ton trucks and drove for miles to witness the continuous mining of potash from the earth's crust. To keep the dust down, the underground roadways were constantly watered.

Potash, a pinky, crystal-like substance, is mined from evaporated underground salt lakes. Standing by the exposed ore body, I was taken by how massive the potash seams were and the relative ease with which I could break pieces off.

With average ore grades in the 20 to 25 percent range, Saskatchewan is the Saudi Arabia of potash. It is home to companies such as PotashCorp (POT—NYSE), Agrium (AGU—NYSE), and Mosaic (MOS—NYSE), which supply almost 39 percent of the world's needs. Even mining giant BHP Billiton Limited (BHP—NYSE) has realized that the economics of potash are just too good to sneeze at. The company has opened an office in downtown Saskatoon, staffed it with more than 200 professionals, and is plotting a path forward to bring these specialty salts to a farm near you.

Roundup

Simply applying commercial fertilizers to a field can result in strong gains in yield. In a previously unfertilized field these gains come quickly and uniformly, but they begin to plateau over time. In this regard, the biggest game changer for farmers has been the introduction of genetically modified (GM) seeds, whose impressive yield gains have altered the competitive dynamic for farming.

~

The biggest game changer for the farmer comes from genetically modified (GM) seeds, whose impressive yield gains have altered the competitive dynamic for farming.

By recombining seed DNA in the laboratory, companies have been able to create seeds that offer superior drought and disease resistance. But the real appeal of these products is their ability to boost the farmer's bottom line by increasing yields and cutting down on the need for costly pesticides and herbicides.

Today, most of America's corn crops are grown with GM seeds, and many believe their use will help to double corn output in the United States by 2030. In Brazil, Argentina, China, and India they've been welcomed with open arms. The European Union, however, has maintained a closed-door policy, banning their use since 1998. Many believe that the human health impacts of GM seeds are still unknown and that trace elements of them can still be detected in the soil years after their use has been discontinued—despite intensive efforts to eradicate them. To detractors, the benefits of the seeds aren't worth the risks.

The undisputed world leader in the biotechnology, or genetic modification, of plants is Monsanto Company (MON—NYSE) of St. Louis, Missouri. And while the debate over the application of GM seeds is likely to persist, Peter Brabeck, the chairman of Nestlé SA, contends that "You cannot feed the world today without genetically modified organisms." With the world of agriculture transitioning from a regional industry to a global one, the inevitable growth in GM seeds will also result in the most sustainable trend in agriculture.

A decade or more of underproduction has set the stage for a surge in profits and prices for all of the agricultural inputs. Moves toward agricultural self-sufficiency, natural limits on the amount of arable land, and population growth will all continue to drive improved agricultural productivity over the next two decades. Farm commercialization will continue to be the best way to boost sagging productivity and is the critical link between stronger tractor sales, rising fertilizer demand, and sales of genetically modified (GM) seeds.

Hot Commodities

- Globally, about one billion people live on a dollar a day—the benchmark for extreme poverty.

- Half the world's grain harvest is fed to livestock, and it's expected that by 2030 another billion metric tons of cereal per year will be required to meet human and animal needs.

- From 1961 to 2005, food production increased at 10 times the rate that arable land became available, as a result of improved agricultural practices.

- With rising incomes, a shift is occurring toward grain- and water-intensive meat-based diets.

- Farm commercialization will be the single biggest factor driving the next decade of growth in agriculture.

- Fertilized crops grow 30 to 50 percent faster than unfertilized crops—giving commercial farms a huge leg up on their small-scale competition.

- Commercial fertilizers act as plant food, delivering various forms of the three critical nutrients (nitrogen, potassium, and phosphate).

- The introduction of GM seeds is altering the competitive dynamic for farmers.

Chapter Eight

Ordering the Breakfast Special

Finding Profits in Foodstuffs

I ALWAYS SAVOR THOSE RARE MORNINGS when I can take the time to enjoy an unhurried breakfast with the newspaper and a steaming-hot cup of coffee. For most of us, that's what breakfast is: an enjoyable way to kick-start the day. But not everyone realizes that behind the typical all-American morning meal of orange juice, eggs, bacon, and coffee lies a thriving global commodity business.

Over the last 11,000 years, from the dawn of agriculture to the opening of the first McDonald's, the story of food has been one of globalization. Steeped in mystery, the spice trade used to be characterized by exotic tales and exorbitant prices; today, of course, every spice imaginable is readily available at your local supermarket. While food is abundant in the West, the country of origin is often a surprise. Coffee, which originated in Ethiopia, and sugar, which first came from New Guinea, are now two of Brazil's dominant exports. Currently, India is the biggest producer of peanuts and China grows the most potatoes, even though both crops originated in South America.

Foodstuffs are no passive indulgence, they're part of a well-balanced commodity portfolio. While copper was the best performing commodity in 2009, rallying more than 150 percent from its December 30, 2008, close, sugar came in second place, with a price move of more than 100 percent. Orange juice, with a price increase of around 45 percent, was also a solid investment during 2009, while cocoa, the bean used to make chocolate, rallied nearly 35 percent over the year. You'll never look at your breakfast special the same way once you perk up to the reality that what you're really staring at is a plateful of potential profits.

Ready for a Perk Up?

Judging from the number of expensive coffee houses in today's metropolises, you'd think that coffee producers had been making out like bandits for years. But most of us *half-caff-latte-with-a-twist* types who've been willingly shelling out the big bucks for our morning indulgence have no idea about the real ups and downs of growing and harvesting coffee beans. Coffee prices have perked up recently, shooting to their highest levels in a decade as rafts of new consumers in India and China develop a taste for a cup of Joe.

Coffee originated in Ethiopia, but was first cultivated in the Arab world. In the 17th century, coffee arrived in Italy before spreading to the rest of Europe and, later, to the Americas. Today, the United States is the largest nation of coffee drinkers in the world.

But coffee is more than just a morning fix, it's a top agricultural export, ranking as the number one export for 12 countries in 2004. Over 100 million people worldwide are dependent on coffee as their primary source of income, and it remains the economic backbone for many African countries, including Ethiopia, Uganda, and Rwanda. However, Brazil is currently the world leader in coffee production. In 2007, its total output was around 2.5 million metric tons, followed by Vietnam, which produced 1.1 million metric tons, and Colombia, which produced 780,000 metric tons.

∽

Coffee originated in Ethiopia, but was first cultivated in the Arab world. Today, America is the world's largest consumer of coffee and Brazil is the largest producer, followed by Vietnam and Colombia.

Two main species of coffee are grown worldwide: *arabica*, the flavorful, milder coffee preferred by many North Americans, and *robusta*, a stronger, more bitter, full-bodied coffee. As it contains about 40 to 50 percent more caffeine, robusta packs a bigger punch than arabica, making it ideal for blending into espresso and as an inexpensive substitute for arabica in commercial coffee blends. Because of its milder flavor, arabica makes up roughly 70 percent of the world's total green coffee production. But no matter what type it is, all coffee comes from the seeds of coffee cherries, which grow on small evergreen shrubs and are usually picked by hand. Coffee cultivation requires lots of water, so coffee shrubs grow best in warm, wet climates; in fact, some have estimated that it takes between 160 to 290 gallons (600 to 1,100 liters) of water to produce just a quarter gallon (one liter) of coffee—which is a big deal for the many coffee-producing nations facing water shortages.

During the mid-1980s, coffee commanded a price of nearly $1.60 per pound; respectable, but still a far cry from its all-time peak of $3.36 per pound in April 1977 (it bottomed at a paltry $0.415 in December 2001). Coffee production has soared over the last few decades as new countries, most notably Vietnam, have entered the market. Big companies like Starbucks may dominate the high-end retail coffee market, but the beans that went into your four-dollar latte were mostly grown by small farming operations in various parts of the world. Coffee growing is backbreaking work. Before the beans can be sold, they must be hand-picked, hauled out of the fields, shelled, dried, and sorted. Nonetheless, carping about the cost of your cappuccino is justified: the actual cost of the beans is mere pennies per cup—far less than milk or beer.

Starbucks has ridden the wave of growing legions of coffee connoisseurs to become the largest coffee chain in the world. But in recent years, over-expansion and rising commodity prices have hit the company's bottom line hard. In 2007, Starbucks' share price fell 42 percent, making it one of the worst performing companies on the NASDAQ. Compounding its problems, *Consumer Reports* magazine, in its March 2007 edition, gave McDonald's filtered coffee a higher rating than Starbucks' pricier alternative. The global economic crisis of 2008–2009 had multitudes of customers defecting to cheaper coffee joints like Dunkin' Donuts, where a daily jolt can be had for about a quarter of the price. To stop the exodus, not to mention the proliferation of negative monikers like "Fourbucks," Starbucks developed Via, an instant coffee aimed at capturing a piece of the $17 billion global instant coffee market. Via was first rolled out in the U.S., yet had Starbucks studied the statistics, it might have concluded that foreign markets were a better place to start: 80 percent of British coffee sales are in instant coffee, versus just 10 percent in America.

Sugar High

The best sugar high you can get these days is from investing in it rather than eating it. After India (the world's second-largest sugar producer) curbed its production by half following low rainfall levels in 2009, sugar prices soared to their highest level in 27 years. India is more than a large producer of sugar—it's also the world's largest consumer of the stuff.

Sugar is believed to have originated in New Guinea, but today sugarcane and sugar beets—the two main sources of those white crystals on your breakfast table— are grown in over 100 countries worldwide. Sugarcane, the source of around 75 percent of all refined sugar, is grown in the tropical and subtropical regions of the world that fall roughly between the Tropics of Capricorn and Cancer. Sugar beets, on the other hand, typically grow best in cooler climates with evenly distributed rainfall. Regardless of whether sugar comes from the beet or the cane though, its chemical composition is identical.

Global production of raw sugar is around 160 million metric tons annually. Brazil is the world's largest producer of sugar, accounting for 20 percent of annual production, and is also the largest exporter—responsible for a staggering 42 percent of world output. Other large sugar producers are India with a 14 percent share, the European Union and Thailand each with 11 percent, and Australia with 8 percent.

~

Global production of raw sugar is around 160 million metric tons annually. Brazil is not only the world's largest producer of sugar, accounting for 20 percent of annual production, but it's also the largest exporter—accounting for a staggering 42 percent of exports.

Brazil's sugar industry is likely to become even more dominant in the years to come, as many of its big companies were forced to merge following the global credit crunch of 2008–2009. Cosan, a company that alone produces 2.5 percent of the world's sugar, snapped up ExxonMobil's Brazilian ethanol distribution business in 2008. In April 2009, French commodity trading house Louis Dreyfus bought Santelisa Vale, a large processor of sugarcane, in a move aimed at bolstering its own sugar trading business. The result of these mergers has been a far more consolidated Brazilian sugar industry, with greater economies of scale and lots of cash to pursue future business expansions.

But Brazil's sugar producers have another edge over the competition. Many can produce ethanol from sugarcane, which serves as a handy backup when world sugar prices are low. Sharp increases in sales of flex-fuel cars, which can run on either gasoline or ethanol, have had the market for ethanol growing at roughly 17 percent per year. It's a good news story that could get a whole lot better if Europe and America ever reduce their tariffs on Brazilian ethanol.

From Grove to Glass

In the 1970s, Florida citrus growers came up with the popular tagline: "A breakfast without orange juice is like a day without sunshine." Nowadays though, it's Brazil, not Florida, that dominates the global orange juice trade. Harnessing a plentiful supply of land and cheap labor,

Brazil has not only become the world's largest orange juice exporter, it also dominates in coffee, beef, and sugar. And unlike many of its rivals, Brazil has room to continue growing as a global agricultural powerhouse—without encroaching on the fragile Amazon rainforest, the country could easily add another 220 million acres (89 million hectares) of farmland to the 148 million acres (60 million hectares) it currently occupies.

Florida may come to mind when you think of orange juice, but it's Brazil, not Florida, that dominates the global orange juice trade.

Originating in Southeast Asia and southern China, oranges have been cultivated for the last 4,000 years. From Asia, oranges migrated to the Middle East where Arab traders helped introduce them throughout the Mediterranean. Spanish and Portuguese explorers brought oranges to the New World. The orange juice industry grew in the 1930s with the development of pasteurization techniques and again later with the widespread use of refrigerators.

There are three main varieties of oranges—Mandarin, Navel, and Valencia—which are often blended to produce a wide variety of flavors. Globally, the orange juice market has annual sales of more than $2.3 billion, with the United States, Canada, Western Europe, and Japan being the largest consumers. In the United States, the Tropicana brand of orange juice reigns supreme, having snagged a 65 percent share of the overall market.

If Florida is big in orange juice, then Brazil is absolutely massive: the country produces 27 percent of the world's oranges, 53 percent of its orange juice, and 50 percent of all frozen concentrated orange juice. The state of São Paulo, in the country's southeast, produces almost all of Brazil's oranges—some 98 percent, grown from 1.7 million acres (688,000 hectares). Florida, by contrast, has seen land dedicated to growing oranges shrink to less than 700,000 acres (283,000 hectares) as population growth increasingly means that land once dedicated to groves is, instead, turned into shopping malls.

~

Brazil produces 27 percent of the world's oranges and 53 percent of all the orange juice consumed globally.

In spite of Brazil's dominance in agricultural commodities, the country faces significant obstacles to boosting output further. Weak institutions, creaking infrastructure, and poor contract enforcement are all challenging its agricultural sector's development. Transportation is also a huge issue. The country's rivers do not crisscross the heart of the country and its rail lines are a shambles. As recently as 2005, just 10 percent of the roads in Brazil were paved—a major impediment to getting food from farm to fork.

Decadent Delight

It's more than a sweet indulgence—it's the world's favorite flavor. Chocolate, which is made from cocoa, is certainly a delightful decadence, but it's also an important traded commodity. The Spanish, who first discovered cocoa in South America more than 500 years ago, called it "the food of the gods." While many would still agree with that assessment today, cocoa's 2009 performance as a commodity investment was equally sweet. Cocoa futures returned 23.4 percent in 2009.

Cocoa, the common name for the powder derived from the seeds of the cacao tree, dates back to the time of the Aztecs. To bring out their chocolate flavor, the seeds must go through the process of being picked, cured, dried in the sun, cleaned, and then roasted. Two-thirds of all cocoa seeds picked today are used to make chocolate. The rest are ground into cocoa powder. The Ivory Coast is the big hammer of cocoa production, supplying 37 percent of the 3.4 million metric tons traded annually. Ghana, another large producer, accounts for 20 percent of global supply, Indonesia produces 14 percent, while Cameroon and Brazil each supply about 5 percent. The biggest sweet tooth belongs to the European Union, which consumes 40 percent of the world's annual cocoa production (versus a mere 12 percent by the U.S.).

~

Two-thirds of cocoa seeds picked are turned into chocolate, while the rest become cocoa powder. The Ivory Coast is the big hammer of coffee production, supplying 37 percent of the 3.4 million metric tons of cocoa traded annually.

But despite soaring cocoa futures, there's trouble lurking in candy land. In Ghana, farm productivity is slumping and the children of many of the country's cocoa farmers aren't interested in working in the family business anymore. For Britain's Cadbury Schweppes, the world's biggest confectioner and now a division of Kraft, this grief from Ghana is bad news given that the country provides *all* of the cocoa for Cadbury's U.K. operations and 70 percent of its global supply. More importantly, Cadbury maintains that it is Ghana's high-quality cocoa that gives their products—including the Creme Egg and the Dairy Milk chocolate bar—their distinctive taste.

In January 2008, the company embarked on a 10-year collaboration with Ghana's cocoa growers, called the "Cadbury Cocoa Partnership," with the aim of boosting cocoa yields by helping cocoa farmers work together better and by encouraging the use of fertilizers.

When Pigs Fly

American pig farmers have had a tough time fattening their wallets lately—rising feed prices, swine flu worries, and a trend toward healthy eating have all impacted their bottom line. And that's been putting pressure on the futures contracts for pork bellies (pork belly is the meat from a pig's belly where bacon comes from), which rallied just 0.72 percent in 2009. In contrast, orange juice futures soared 80.9 percent the same year. Normally, the strongest time for pork bellies sales is the fiscal second quarter when barbeques start firing up. Lately, however, this seasonal custom hasn't been enough to support sagging sales.

As the world's third-largest producer (and biggest exporter) of pork and pork products, America is particularly vulnerable to fluctuations in the global pork trade. When the global economy slumped sharply in 2009, exports faltered, and suddenly far fewer American pigs found themselves going to market. China, the largest consumer of pork in the world, cut back dramatically on its consumption during the financial crisis. In the U.S., pork exports to China all but dried up in May of 2009—down nearly 96 percent from May 2008 levels.

As the world's third-largest producer and biggest exporter of pork and pork products, America is particularly vulnerable to the global trade in pork.

Pig farmers weren't the only ones taking it on the chin in 2009, however, so too were the pork producers. In June, Virginia-based Smithfield Foods, the world's largest producer and processor of pork, posted its first loss in more than 30 years. With nearly 67 million head of swine in the U.S. slurping at the trough, pork meat was soon piling up on supermarket shelves. Because cheap pork competes with beef, particularly the expensive cuts, the growing backlog also put downward pressure on beef prices. America, which has the largest grain-fed cattle industry in the world, is extremely sensitive to the downturns in pork prices that result when consumers switch to cheaper meat cuts. And since the majority of American beef is corn-fed, the country's corn-based ethanol program has also increased margin pressure for cattle farmers. In spite of its industry's size, the U.S.

still imports beef, albeit mostly a lower-value grass-fed product that later gets turned into ground beef.

The situation for poultry hasn't been much better. In response to higher grain prices and slumping sales in 2008, poultry producers began cutting back on production. Unfortunately for Pilgrim's Pride, America's largest chicken producer, the change came a little too late: the company filed for bankruptcy protection in December of the same year.

A Plateful of Profits

The easiest, most direct method of creating your very own breakfast special is to choose one of the many food-stuff-linked commodity ETFs. Oh sure, you could buy shares in Kraft Foods Inc. (KFT—NYSE) or Nestlé SA (NESN VX—SIX), the Swiss food powerhouse, but then you'd be buying into a food conglomerate. Although food conglomerates can do well when their brands are strong, keep in mind that growth is often hard to come by. In a bid to boost sales and jump-start sluggish growth, Nestlé is currently embarking on a shift towards health and nutrition businesses and away from slower growth food-stuffs. The company already owns Jenny Craig, the chain of weight-loss centers, and is hoping to add products catering to a more affluent, health-conscious consumer.

But while the concept may be sound, turning an aircraft carrier of a business like Nestlé around won't be easy. If the effort fails, the consequences for the company's well-established brands could be disastrous.

The easiest and most direct method of creating your very own breakfast special is to choose one of the many foodstuff-linked commodity ETFs.

A single-commodity ETF is a far better way to play the foodstuffs than wading through a quagmire of earnings reports and investor presentations. U.K.-based ETF Securities offers several excellent pure-play commodity ETFs, such as ETFS Sugar (SUGA), ETFS Lean Hogs (HOGS), and ETFS Coffee (COFF), which all trade on the London Stock Exchange (LSE).

A combination of factors, including inefficient and small-scale farming, a concentrated number of major producing countries, and a global population boom, will result in higher prices in the years to come. With supply squeezed tighter than the oranges in your daily glass of juice, prices for commodity foodstuffs can only increase. Once you perk up to the investment opportunities sitting right on your plate, you'll never think of breakfast as just food again.

Hot Commodities

- Foodstuffs such as coffee, sugar, orange juice, and cocoa are major traded commodities that have been on a tear lately.

- Coffee originated in Ethiopia, but was first cultivated in the Arab world. Today, America is the world's largest coffee consumer and Brazil is the largest producer, followed by Vietnam and Colombia.

- Global production of raw sugar is around 160 million metric tons annually. Brazil is not only the world's largest producer of sugar, it's also the largest exporter—accounting for a staggering 42 percent of global sugar exports.

- Florida may come to mind when you think of orange juice, but it's Brazil that dominates the global orange juice trade.

- Brazil produces 27 percent of the world's oranges and 53 percent of all the orange juice consumed globally.

- Two-thirds of cocoa seeds are turned into chocolate, while the rest become cocoa powder. The Ivory Coast is the big hammer of coffee production, supplying 37 percent of the 3.4 million metric tons of cocoa traded annually.

- Despite having the largest beef cattle industry in the world, America is still a net importer of beef.

- The U.S. is the third-largest pork producer and the world's largest pork-exporting nation.

- The easiest, most direct method of creating your very own breakfast special is by investing in one of the many foodstuff-linked commodity ETFs.

Chapter Nine

Gaining in Grains

⁓

Investing in Grains

AGRICULTURE HAS A WELL-DESERVED REPUTATION as a cyclical business. It wasn't immune to the 2008–2009 financial crisis, as plummeting prices for grains like rice, wheat, soybeans, and corn demonstrated. Still, grains held up much better than most other commodities—today they remain 30 to 50 percent above their price averages of the past decade. What's more, investor interest in the sector is up sharply as savvy traders correctly reason that, no matter how bad things get, people still need to eat.

Helping to propel grain prices higher these days are the shifting diets of millions of people in the developing world. China's impact alone on global grain consumption has been profound. From 2000 to 2009, China's consumption of wheat increased by 25 percent, beef by more than 30 percent, poultry by 60 percent, and vegetable oil by 100 percent.

Food for Thought

One of my summertime pleasures is eating fresh corn on the cob drizzled with melted butter and a touch of salt. But corn is more than just a summer treat: it's big business. Used primarily for animal and human consumption, corn is the single most valuable crop grown in the United States. The U.S. produces other feed grains such as barley, oats, and sorghum, but corn, which accounts for more than 90 percent of total feed-grain production, rules the roost. Demand for corn has risen with increases in global livestock numbers and with the passage of federal legislation mandating the use of corn-based ethanol, which now laps up 30 percent of U.S. corn production. With around 80 million acres (32 milion hectares) of farmland (mostly in the Midwest) dedicated to corn, the U.S. is the world's largest producer and exporter of the grain.

Corn may be the number one crop in the U.S., but soybeans, a valuable oilseed used in the production of vegetable oil, come in a close second. Soybeans are often grown in rotation with corn, so it should come as no surprise that America is also their largest producer and exporter. Tofu and other soy-based foods are increasingly popular these days, yet the vast majority of soybeans grown in the U.S. aren't consumed by health-conscious yuppies. Instead, they're crushed to produce vegetable oil while the remaining meal is fed to cattle and other livestock. Although canola oil is gaining in popularity, most cooking oils used in the U.S. are still made from soybeans—accounting for 55 to 65 percent of all vegetable oils consumed there.

Although the U.S. is the hammer in the global corn trade and the biggest single producer of soybeans, its dominance in all things soy has been challenged lately by a couple of upstarts from South America—Argentina and Brazil—which have experienced a phenomenal rise in terms of both production and exports. Together, these two countries now represent more than half the total export market, up sharply from just 15 percent in 1980.

Seeds of Doubt

Low-carbohydrate diets may be all the rage in South Beach, but they aren't too popular with the American wheat farmer. Demand for wheat is closely tied to the overall demand for breads and other baked goods made from wheat flour. In the U.S., wheat demand peaked at 225 pounds (102 kilograms) per person per year way back in 1879, declining to around 137 pounds (62 kilograms) today—the result of changing consumer tastes combined with a general societal shift from physically demanding manual labor to office-based work. While wheat is still an important field crop, it ranks a distant third behind corn and soybeans in terms of both acreage and farm receipts. Farmers, discouraged by foreign competition and the poor economics of wheat relative to other crops, have slashed the acreage dedicated to its production by nearly one-third since 1981.

∼

American farmers, discouraged by foreign competition and poor economics relative to other crops, have slashed acreage dedicated to wheat production by nearly one-third since 1981.

The international wheat market is fragmented; no single country dominates production. This, along with seasonally balanced production from both the northern and southern hemispheres, has resulted in wheat prices that are relatively stable over time. The U.S. is the largest wheat-exporting nation, despite producing just 10 percent of the worldwide supply. Other large wheat exporters include Canada, Russia, Kazakhstan, Australia, and Argentina. Wheat is consumed all around the world, but Japan, Brazil, and South Korea are some of the biggest wheat importers.

You Reap What You Sow

No grain is more steeped in tradition and mystique than rice. A staple for half the world's population, rice is consumed daily by more than three billion people across Asia and Africa. In Japan, rice is more than food: it's a symbol of humility and harmony—qualities revered in that country. Rice actually served as a unit of taxation in Japan throughout most of the Middle Ages, and the farmers who produced it had a high social standing. Today, rice is still central to Japanese culture, and rice farming is a heavily subsidized and coddled industry.

Some 440 million metric tons of rice are produced globally every year, making it the second largest staple crop behind corn. Rice is produced all over the world, but for optimal growth it requires plenty of water and high average temperatures. U.S. rice comes from irrigated fields, making America one of the highest-cost (in terms of water, fertilizer, and fuel) and highest-yielding rice producers. The U.S. rice market has doubled since the mid-1980s, partly due to the influx and influence of Asian immigrants.

But in spite of the growth in American consumption, the U.S. produces less than 2 percent of the world's rice and exports nearly half of its production. America may have a modest share of global rice production, but because the international rice trade is so small, America accounts for 10 percent of the global rice trade. In Arkansas, rice paddies cover nearly 1.5 million acres (607,000 hectares) and are the state's main farm export, contributing about $1.6 billion to the economy. Many of the state's 20,000 rice workers are employed at Riceland Foods, the world's largest miller and marketer of the grain.

Rice, like food and farming generally, is sensitive to the politics of the countries where it is produced. Recent events in Venezuela offer a case in point. In early 2009, a Venezuelan rice plant belonging to Cargill, an American company, was *temporarily* seized for violating the country's so-called food security law, while a pasta plant, a tuna-cannery, and several farms were taken over by troops and ordered to concentrate on making price-controlled goods. President Hugo Chávez justified these assaults on the private sector and its capitalist business model with the rallying cry: "Let us construct a new logic, that of socialism."

~

The U.S. produces less than 2 percent of the world's rice and exports nearly half of its production—accounting for 10 percent of the global rice trade.

Sweet Home Chicago

Farming is a cyclical business that certainly has its fair share of ups and downs. Bad weather can destroy a farmer's crops and finances without warning. A bountiful harvest can mean abundant grain supplies but depressed wheat prices. Uncertain volumes and prices can also be a big problem for food processing companies and other middlemen who need to buy crops for their own operations.

As far back as 1848, businessmen and farmers in the Chicago area recognized this problem and believed the formation of a futures exchange could be part of the solution. Chicago was a growing city located at the heart of the U.S. Midwest. With vital rail and shipping links, it seemed like a logical location. And so it was that the Chicago Board of Trade was born, creating a place for farmers to sell their *future* grain crops forward to buyers looking to lock-in the price of grain.

Chicago Bulls

Agricultural trading is no gentleman's pastime. Rather, it's a rough and tumble world where loud, beefy men from Chicago's gritty south side face off against one another—jostling, shoving, and shouting their wagers in a trading pit where the traditional open outcry method is used to match up buyers and sellers of agricultural commodities. Facilitating the betting on the prospective price of everything from next year's weather to the price of wheat, the Chicago Board of Trade and the sharp-elbowed traders who work in its trading pits are front and center in the world of commodities.

For years Chicago was home to two cross-town rivals—the Chicago Mercantile Exchange (CME) and the Chicago Board of Trade (CBOT)—which competed for control of the lucrative exchange-traded futures market. More than 70 percent of the world's grain derivatives, a fast-growing area of finance, are traded at the CBOT, the older of the two exchanges. But in spite of the two exchanges' heft in futures, options, and other derivative products, both have been dominated by small trading shops ("locals") that control most of their seats. At the CBOT, for example, three-quarters of its 1,402 seats had historically been controlled by small grain-trading businesses and retirees who love exploiting the inefficiencies of the market.

For much of their existence, the sleepy, backward nature of open outcry exchanges like the CBOT worked fine. The locals loved the profits and the gruff camaraderie that came from exploiting small, arcane futures markets like those for wheat and soybeans. But agriculture has increasingly caught the attention of the world's biggest investors who have, in turn, demanded greater market efficiency. The CBOT and the CME have also faced competition in their traditional businesses from newer, more flexible electronic exchanges, such as the Intercontinental Exchange (ICE), which are cheaper to establish and offer customers lower transaction costs. The CBOT's electronic Treasury-bond futures market trades more contracts and makes more money than the traditional floor trading of grain. Yet in spite of electronic trading's obvious virtues, the CBOT, and many other open outcry exchanges, have been steadfastly resistant to progress. In the face of these pressures, and with trillions of dollars worth of daily trading at stake, the CME snapped up its former rival, the CBOT, for $8.9 billion in the summer of 2007.

But for the CME, total domination of the world's futures exchanges was not to come until 2008, when, in a bold move, CME Group boss Craig Donohue negotiated the takeover of the New York Mercantile Exchange (NYMEX). Today, the CME Group is the world's largest and most valuable derivatives exchange, trading everything from contracts for oil and corn to U.S. Treasury debt. With more than $4 trillion worth of daily contracts and 95 percent of American futures trading under a single roof, the CME Group is one dominant Chicago bull.

~

With more than $4 trillion worth of daily contracts and 95 percent of American futures trading under a single roof, the CME Group is one dominant Chicago bull.

Grain and Bear It

Prices for grains have been rising lately, driven by increased global demand for food, feed, and fuel. Additionally, critical stockpiles of cereals (rice, wheat, and other coarse grains) are near record lows and Wall Street is betting heavily on agricultural futures—both of which have also sent grain prices higher. In the U.S., investment activity linked to the buying of crop futures was responsible for fully *half* of the rise in the prices of corn, wheat, and soybeans in 2007. And because the U.S. is the largest exporting nation of all these grains, speculative activity on American exchanges helps to drive global grain prices even higher.

From January 2006 through April 2008, index fund investment activity in CBOT wheat, soybeans, and corn futures rose 66 percent. Over the same time period, investments in livestock and grain futures more than doubled to $65 billion from $25 billion, according to AgResource Co., a research firm based in Chicago. Institutional investors have been drawn to the crops markets, in part because they are thinly traded and subject to shortages—a situation that can help drive crop prices sharply higher. The grains markets' unusually small size can also cause price distortions: only 20 percent of the world's wheat production is traded, and only 7 percent of rice production is exported, let alone exchange traded.

⁓

The grains markets' unusually small size can also cause price distortions: only 20 percent of the world's wheat production is traded, and only 7 percent of rice production is exported, let alone exchange traded.

International benchmark prices for grains can also be distorted by small shifts in supply and demand in key exporting countries. World corn prices and trade are largely dependent on weather in the U.S. Midwest. A drought affecting U.S. corn production might result in higher domestic prices, for example, but it will certainly lead to sharp cutbacks in the 20 percent of corn intended for export—a move that would cause prices to soar. Small export volumes for the key global grains often result in prices that are higher internationally than domestically.

Food Chain

Rising grain prices impact not only the price of your daily bread, but also the cost of milk and meat. Soybeans, corn, and wheat are used for cattle and pig feed, therefore, any rise in grain prices directly affects beef and pork prices. By some estimates, a 30 percent rise in grain prices translates into a 10 percent increase in livestock prices (with a three- to six-month lag). But even that may be underestimating the impact of grain prices on America's beef and poultry industries, considering that corn feed represents about two-thirds of the input costs for the beef industry alone. While rising grain prices may be a good news story for grain farmers, they're definitely a bad news story for ranchers and poultry producers.

―――――――― ∽ ――――――――

Corn feed represents about two-thirds of the input costs for the U.S. beef industry. While rising grain prices may be a good news story for grain farmers, they're definitely a bad news story for ranchers and poultry producers.

Weather Report

Inventory levels, weather conditions, and supply and demand in key exporting countries all impact the grain market. Since the beginning of time, farmers have planted their crops according to the seasons, but lately the seasons have been anything but certain. British charity Oxfam has recently reported a litany of weather-related complaints from small farmers around the world, including shorter, more violent rainy seasons and shrinking periods of more moderate temperatures. The International Food Policy Research Institute (IFPRI), a Washington think tank, has cited climate change as the major reason for these dramatic changes. One of their sobering conclusions is that by 2050 global crop yields could be just *half* of 2000 levels, which would present a massive problem if, as expected, the global population expands by 50 percent over the same time frame.

In India, where agriculture accounts for just 18 percent of GDP but 60 percent of employment, lack of rain can be devastating. Planting is usually planned for the summer months, when 80 percent of India's rain normally falls. However, between June and mid-August 2009, there were 29 percent fewer monsoons than average. In India, agriculture accounts for 18 percent of GDP, but employs 60 percent of Indians, making this a very tough pill to swallow.

In 2008, following a cold spring, the state of Iowa had the opposite problem—it received too much rain. By mid-June 2008, Governor Chet Culver had assigned disaster designations to 83 of 99 counties after 16 percent of the state's tillable acres were left under water. It was dubbed by some as the "Great Flood of 2008." And for Iowa, the largest producer of corn and soybeans in the United States, the summer was a bust. But sometimes out of disaster comes opportunity. After the U.S. Department of Agriculture forecast that 43 percent of that year's corn crop would be in fair to poor condition, corn futures for July 2008 jumped to $7.46 per bushel on June 18, 2008, up 27 percent from the May 19, 2008, price of $5.87 per bushel.

Plowing for Profits

Record low stockpiles, changing diets, erratic weather patterns, and a greater number of mouths to feed will result in higher grain prices in the years to come. But not only are grains a profitable investment niche to exploit on their own, they also serve another critical function: as lead indicators for fertilizer investments. Higher grain prices mean fatter pockets for farmers, who are always looking for ways to maximize their profits. Of course, improving yields through increased fertilization is a slam dunk, but farmers—a notoriously frugal bunch—generally wait until they have cash in hand before they spend it.

———————————————— ∽ ————————————————

Grains are not only a profitable investment niche to exploit on their own, but they serve another critical function—they act as a leading indicator for fertilizer investments.

A large capitalization, pure-play grain stock is about as rare as July snowflakes in Texas. One stock that does give you broad exposure to the agricultural industry is Archer Daniels Midland (ADM—NYSE). A global giant operating in 60 countries on six continents, ADM processes grains into value-added products used by the food, beverage, and animal feed industries and is also involved in the production of biofuels. Additionally, the company's Agricultural Services division operates an international network of grain elevators and transportation services to store, clean, and bring grains to market. Wherever you look along the agricultural food chain, from field to table, ADM is there.

———————————————— ∽ ————————————————

A large capitalization, pure-play grain stock is about as rare as July snowflakes in Texas.

Another company that spans the food chain by providing everything from fertilizers to food products is Bunge Limited (BG—NYSE). Like ADM, Bunge has a large agribusiness that buys, stores, and sells grains around the world. But unlike ADM, Bunge has a strong focus on South America, particularly Brazil—making it much more dependent on agricultural trends in that part of the world.

There's even an ETF, the PowerShares DB Agriculture Fund[*] (DBA—NYSE), that offers broad exposure to grains, as well as cattle, cotton, cocoa, and hogs. The fund buys agricultural futures and is designed to mimic the returns of the Deutsche Bank Liquid Commodity Index—an agricultural index calibrated to reflect the overall performance of the sector.

Floods, famine, and food all impact the business of agriculture. But as the world's population grows and diets change, the demand for high protein food will only increase, underpinning strong demand for grains. Agriculture may be a cyclical business, but grain prices have nevertheless exhibited the greatest stability of all the commodities over the last decade. After all, eating is something we all need to do.

---

[*] On January 19, 2010, the weighting towards grains, soybean oil, and soybean meal was 34.3 percent.

Hot Commodities

- Shifting diets and economic growth in the developing world are behind a general rise in the prices of most grains.

- Corn and soybeans are the big cash crops grown in America, with wheat a distant third.

- Rice is the world's second largest staple crop. America produces less than 2 percent of the world's rice and exports nearly half of its production—accounting for 10 percent of the global rice trade.

- Chicago is the global epicenter of grain trading.

- The CME Group trades more than $4 trillion worth of contracts daily, in everything from oil to corn, and controls 95 percent of America's exchange-traded futures market.

- The grains markets are amongst the smallest of all commodity markets, a situation that can sometimes distort prices. Only 20 percent of the world's wheat production is traded and only 7 percent of rice production is exported, let alone exchange traded.

- Corn feed represents about two-thirds of the input costs for the American beef industry, so when grain prices are high, beef and poultry producers' margins come under pressure.

- Grains are not only a profitable investment niche to exploit on their own, they also act as a leading indicator for fertilizer investments.

- A large capitalization, pure-play grain stock is extremely rare.

- A growing world population and changing diets will underpin strong demand for grains.

- Grains are among the least cyclical of all commodities because eating is something we all need to do.

Chapter Ten

Bulk Up

~

Benefitting from Bulk Commodities

NOTHING SAYS INDUSTRIALIZATION like the steel industry. Steel is produced all over the world and is seen as a key industrial pillar because it provides the necessary raw materials for prestige industries such as appliance and automobile manufacturing. Since the 1850s, steel has been inexorably linked to the industrial economy and has remained front and center there as nations have continued to industrialize. Whether in America at the turn of the 20th century, in Japan and South Korea after the Second World War, or in China and India today—where there's industry, there's sure to be steel.

Cheap Thrills

As I stood on the catwalk, 100 yards away from the massive electric arc furnace at Lake Ontario Steel, I could feel a cold sweat moving down my back. After the last load of car parts had been emptied into the 850,000-metric-ton furnace, the operator closed the lid and three massive graphite electrodes were lowered into place. Soon an enormous electrical charge would flow to the graphite electrodes, striking a massive arc within the furnace and melting the scrap steel at temperatures in excess of 3,272 degrees Fahrenheit (1,800 degrees Celsius). The heat, noise, sparks, and sheer brutal physical power that would be unleashed for a few short minutes, transforming old car parts into steel billets, struck a primal nerve with me.

Little did I know then that my experience as a junior plant engineer 20 years earlier would help me to understand one of the most important and fiercely nationalistic of all industries. When steel mills around the world are producing round rebar and flat rolled steel for car manufacturing plants and construction projects, it's a sure sign that industrial production is on the rebound.

Fire and Brimstone

I've always loved the fire-and-brimstone primitivism of the steel industry, not to mention the heavy dose of superstition that goes along with it—attributes that used to contribute to the industry's legendary inefficiency. Lake Ontario Steel, for example, used to pay its rolling mill foreman a handsome salary for the core skill of *hearing* when one mill stand was pushing a billet too fast or too slow. Of course, that was before the company decided to spend millions on a Siemens speed-control system aimed at taking the guesswork out of forming the finished structural steel shapes!

Steel is an alloy containing 97 percent iron plus carbon and other metals (such as zinc or chromium) and is produced in a basic oxygen furnace (BOF) or, in the case of recycled steel, in an electric arc furnace. Access to plenty of scrap steel and low electricity prices have helped make America the primary home of electric arc steelmaking technology.

The recipe for producing steel in a basic oxygen furnace is straightforward: combine between one- and three-quarter metric tons of molten iron ore with three-quarters of a metric ton of coke (processed metallurgical coal), a quarter metric ton of limestone, and four metric tons of air, crank up the heat to 3,500 degrees Fahrenheit

(1,297 degrees Celsius) and presto! Soon you've got raw steel that can be reheated later and rolled into a wide variety of shapes and sizes. Mini-mills, which melt scrap steel in an electric arc furnace, are the fastest growing method of production today, having increased their market share from 15 to 31 percent over the last two decades. But in spite of this rapid growth, integrated steel mills that utilize the BOF steelmaking technology produce a higher quality end product and account for over 66 percent of global steel production.

***

Integrated steel mills that utilize the BOF steelmaking technology produce a higher quality end product and account for over 66 percent of global steel production.

Growth in Girders

No city symbolizes the rise and fall of America's steel industry better than Pittsburgh. With its strategic location at the intersection of the Monongahela, Allegheny, and Ohio rivers and smack in the middle of one of the nation's most productive coalfields, Pittsburgh's destiny was always steel. By the end of the American Civil War, the city was producing more than half of the nation's steel. Industrialists such as Andrew Mellon, Henry Clay Frick, and Andrew Carnegie built their fortunes there. Yet by the 1970s and 1980s, Pittsburgh's steel industry was in decline, besieged by competition from cheap overseas product. With the collapse of the American steel industry in the 1980s, Pittsburgh lost more than 120,000 jobs, amounting to more than half of its manufacturing positions.

Enter the Dragon

China emerged as the new sheriff in steel country after producing 37.1 percent of the alloy's global output in 2007, a sharp increase from the 15.3 percent it produced in 2000. China's love affair with steel dates back all the way to the Han Dynasty, 1,800 years ago, when primitive forms of it were produced. Today, China, known as the world's factory, boasts more than 700 steel mills and nearly 7,000 companies involved in bending, shaping, or otherwise forming steel. China's steel output is so plentiful that, by the government's estimation, it produces more than 100 million metric tons of *surplus* steel per year—an amount greater than the entire U.S. production.

As foreign investment has flowed in, China's steel industry has grown by leaps and bounds, increasing by more than 20 percent a year over the last decade alone. Today, China produces more steel than Brazil, Russia,

Ukraine, Germany, India, South Korea, and the United States *combined*.

Today, China produces more steel than Brazil, Russia, Ukraine, Germany, India, South Korea, and the United States *combined*.

To consolidate their political power and increase regional revenues, provincial and local officials in China eagerly court the steel industry—sometimes even leaning on banks to make loans to the industry. Today, a patchwork quilt of steel mills has sprung up all over the country, resulting in half a dozen major steel-producing provinces and more than a dozen smaller provinces all vying to out-produce one another. The result is a highly balkanized, inefficient industry where the top three steel producers account for only 20 percent of total production. In South Korea, by contrast, two enormous mills account for 87 percent of total steel output.

Let the Good Times Roll

The global steel industry rolls out more than 1.3 billion metric tons of hot rolled coils, sheets, plates, rounds, rebar, and various other products annually. Unfortunately, a mix of national pride, provincial politics, and the desire to drive industrial expansion into prestige manufacturing has made the industry extremely fragmented. In copper mining, for instance, the top 10 producers control more than 57 percent of global mine supplies, whereas in steel production, the top 10 global players accounted for just 27 percent of world production at the end of 2007.

———————————— ∽ ————————————

In copper mining, for instance, the top 10 producers control more than 57 percent of global mine supplies, whereas in steel production, the top 10 global players accounted for just 27 percent of world production at the end of 2007.

One company bucking the trend and going global is ArcelorMittal, the largest steel company in the world, representing around 10 percent of global output. By organizing his company along global rather than nationalistic lines, Indian-born tycoon Lakshmi Mittal has managed to turn the sleepy national steel company model on its head. Steel began to decline in the West when every country, regardless of its ability to compete, decided it *had to have* its own national steel giant. The result was a spate of money-losing government-owned mills that couldn't compete with newer, more efficient operations in low-wage countries. By attracting global talent, rather than local flunkies, and offering training at its own university in Luxembourg, ArcelorMittal has created a truly global company culture—amongst its top 30 managers, nine different nationalities are represented. Mittal has ultimately succeeded in doing what others have tried and failed to do: build the steel industry's only truly global producer.

Grist for the Mill

A constant supply of iron is needed to keep the world's blast furnaces operating at full tilt. Luckily, iron ore, or iron-bearing rock, is relatively plentiful—it constitutes 5 percent of the earth's crust. Iron is the world's most commonly used metal, with 98 percent of all iron ore earmarked for steelmaking. Steel, of course, is the backbone of the modern economy and a key component in cars, ships, buildings, and machinery. From 2002 to 2008, iron ore prices shot up fourfold, fuelled by strong global growth, in particular from China. While Japan and South Korea are considered huge iron ore consumers, China, the world's largest steel producer, is a whale of a buyer, snapping up more than half of all iron ore exports.

~

Iron is the world's most commonly used metal, with 98 percent of all iron ore earmarked for steelmaking.

Luckily for China, it's not only the world's biggest consumer of iron ore, but also its largest producer. But in spite of China's dominance as a producer of iron ore, its demand is so massive that it is reliant on imports to keep its steel mills humming. Other major producers are Australia, Brazil, India, and Russia. In total, the world produces about one billion metric tons of ore annually, with production dominated internationally by three firms: BHP Billiton, Rio Tinto, and Vale.

China continues to transform itself by investing massively in infrastructure, and iron ore is the most vital of all the raw materials that China needs to keep its economic juggernaut moving full steam ahead. Lately Chinese officials have tried to overturn the iron ore oligopoly by encouraging Chinese companies to negotiate collectively and by buying stakes in iron ore producers.

In 2008, China's state-controlled aluminum firm, Chinalco, bought a 9 percent stake in Australia's Rio Tinto. At the time, Rio Tinto, reeling from the collapse of commodity markets and from massive debts incurred from its 2007 acquisition of Canada's Alcan, welcomed the investment. But as commodity prices improved in 2009 and Chinalco decided to raise its stake to 18 percent, Rio Tinto's shareholders suddenly balked. Rather than accepting Chinalco's investment, Rio Tinto reneged on the deal it had made with the Chinese aluminum giant and instead formed a joint venture with fellow Anglo-Australian mining giant BHP Billiton. Under this new arrangement, the two mining companies agreed to merge their operations in Western Australia in an attempt to further concentrate their dominant position over the world's iron ore business.

Risky Business

Prices for iron ore are set once a year in annual negotiations. The first price agreed to between a big Japanese, South Korean, or Chinese steelmaker and one of the big three mining giants sets the benchmark for all other buyers and sellers to follow. In recent years, rocketing Chinese demand for iron ore has meant sky-high prices and has turned the annual negotiations into an eagerly watched spectator sport.

In July 2009, things took a dramatic twist, however, when Chinese authorities arrested four Rio Tinto employees and two Chinese steel company employees and accused them of overcharging for iron ore by a whopping $102.5 billion over a six-year period. It likely wasn't a coincidence that these developments came shortly after Rio Tinto rejected Chinalco's additional investment and just before the annual iron ore contract negotiations were set to begin.

Soot and Success

It's probably a long time since you've heard anything about chimney sweeps, but, believe it or not, coal was the fastest growing fossil fuel of the last century—the Asia Pacific region alone accounted for 90 percent of the demand growth. As a source of global energy, coal should not be underestimated: it supplied 27 percent of the world's needs in 2009, just behind oil at 36 percent. And the International Energy Agency recently predicted that demand will grow at 1.9 percent through to 2015, meaning that coal would outpace the growth of all other fossil fuels except natural gas.

Coal was the fastest growing fossil fuel of the last century—with the Asia Pacific region accounting for 90 percent of the demand growth.

Coal comes in two different forms: metallurgical coal, which is converted into coke for use in steelmaking, and thermal coal, which is used in coal-fired electricity generation. Of the seven billion short tons of coal that are mined annually throughout the world, 60 percent comes from underground mines. The vast majority of coal that is produced (roughly 85 percent of global mine production, or six billion short tons) is the thermal coal used in power plants. Metallurgical coal, used in steel production, is less abundant and comes from high-quality deposits in the eastern United States, Western Canada, and Australia.

The Powder River Basin (PRB) in Wyoming and Montana is the single largest coal-producing region in the U.S. and the fastest growing coal region in America. I remember standing in one of Arch Coal's (ACI—NYSE) surface mines in Wyoming and marveling at how large the coal seam was. Three or four feet thick and stretching as far as the eye could see, the coal seam was quite easy to spot; it was not only massive, but its blackness and smooth texture made it easy to distinguish from the surrounding rock. Mining operations are some of the coolest things you can see. Perhaps it's just the engineer in me, but I always marvel at the speed and complexity of operations such as Arch's. For today's bulk mining companies, these massive material handling operations are all in a day's work. The other big coal-producing areas in the U.S. are Central and Northern Appalachia, which, when combined with PRB coal, account for 75 percent of U.S. mine output. The biggest consumer of U.S. coal is, far and away, the electric power industry, which consumed 93 percent of domestic coal production in 2007.

~

**The biggest consumer of U.S. coal is, far
and away, the electric power industry, which
consumed 93 percent of the domestic coal
production in 2007.**

G'Day Mate

In Australia, coal is a big deal. Coal was first mined in
Newcastle in 1797, and ever since then Australians have
been reliant on it as a cheap and abundant source of
energy. Australia is the world's biggest coal exporter, and
the black stuff pouring through the port of Newcastle
has become a vital economic linchpin for the economy,
accounting for one-fifth of its foreign earnings in 2007.
It's also become the critical link for power generation
there, with 83 percent of the country's electricity coming from coal-fired generation. On the downside, coal
dependence has made Australia one of the world's biggest
emitters of carbon dioxide. This has caused a headache
for Prime Minister Kevin Rudd, who's had to scramble
to find common ground between environmentalists and
the coal mining industry, which argues that Rudd's pro-
posed cap-and-trade policy would unfairly penalize it by

allowing other countries to leapfrog ahead of Australia in the global coal markets.

Indonesia, already the world's largest supplier of thermal coal, potentially stands to benefit from all of Australia's environmental handwringing. Demand for coal has grown rapidly as the Asian economies have expanded, and Indonesia has found itself at the heart of the boom. China may be the largest producer of coal in the world, but it's often cheaper for it to import coal from Indonesia rather than to rail it from its own interior; not only is Indonesian coal less expensive, but its quality is better too. Eighty percent of China's electricity comes from coal. And that's great news for Indonesia, which exported 190 million of the 230 million metric tons of the coal it produced in 2009.

The seaborne, or export, market for coal is small, currently accounting for just 13 percent of the global market, or 885 million metric tons (metallurgical coal represents about one quarter of this). While demand for coal of all types continues to grow, exports have been slow to respond and are often hampered by insufficient port and rail capacity in large coal-exporting countries such as South Africa, Colombia, and Australia. In Newcastle, the busiest coal port in the world, miles-long queues of freighters waiting to top up their holds with coal have become a common sight.

~

The seaborne, or export, market for coal is small—accounting for just 13 percent of the global market. Insufficient port and rail capacity has hampered the growth of the export market.

Ships Ahoy

Iron ore, coal, steel, and other bulk raw materials used as inputs for finished and semi-finished goods all have to be transported by sea. There's only a set number of large ships in the world and, with a couple of years' lag time to bring on any new ones, freight rates move up and down quickly in response to changes in demand. Thankfully, you don't need a savvy uncle in the ship brokering business to keep tabs on global shipping rates—all you need to know is what's happening with the Baltic Dry Index (BDI).

~

To keep tabs on global shipping rates, you don't need a savvy uncle in the ship brokering business—all you need to know is what's happening with the Baltic Dry Index (BDI).

To compile its daily index, the London-based Baltic Exchange canvasses brokers around the globe to find out the cost of shipping various cargoes. The BDI compiles the associated costs of shipping dry bulk commodities (grain, iron ore, coal, etc.) by Handymax, Panamax, and Capesize ships along 26 routes. Between June and October of 2008, the index tumbled more than 90 percent when Lehman Brothers went bust and the world economy imploded. And as the world economy continued to fizzle, the cost of moving a standard container from China to Europe slid from $1,400 to $400. Investors can rest assured that when the global economy shifts back into high gear, cargo rates—and the Baltic Index—will be heading higher.

Forget the Future

When shipping rates rise, investors should increase their exposure to bulk commodities such as iron ore, steel, and coal. But unlike most other commodities, there isn't an iron ore or coal futures contract that the eager investor can trade. Luckily, it's possible to increase your exposure to "the bulks" by loading up on the companies that supply these critical raw materials to the global marketplace. The global big daddies of iron ore are BHP Billiton (BHP—NYSE), Rio Tinto (RTP—NYSE), and

Vale (VALE–NYSE), all of which trade as American Depositary Shares (ADS) on the NYSE.

Unlike most other commodities, there isn't an iron ore or coal futures contract that eager investors can trade.

A smart way to gain access to the one-trillion-dollar global steel market is through shares of companies that supply the metallurgical coal ("met coal") used in steelmaking. Investment bank Morgan Stanley sees BHP Billiton as *the* big hammer in global metallurgical coal, given that it supplied 32 percent of the seaborne market in 2006. But an up-and-comer for investors to consider is the number two supplier to the seaborne met market: Teck Resources Ltd. (TCK–NYSE), which also happens to be Canada's largest diversified mining company and the operator of Elk Valley Coal.

Another great way to get exposure to the global steel market is to buy shares in the better quality steel producers. The largest, and arguably the best, steelmaker in the world is ArcelorMittal (MT–NYSE). Those looking to stay a little closer to home might also consider investing in U.S. Steel Corporation (X–NYSE). Despite being a fraction of its former size and just the 10th largest steel producer in the world, U.S. Steel, and other companies that produce bulk commodities, will still be on the move when global industrial production begins to roar.

Hot Commodities

- Steel, an important industrial pillar that supports prestige industries, is produced the world over.

- Steel can be made in either an electric arc furnace (using scrap steel) or in a basic oxygen furnace (using raw materials), which produces a higher-quality end product.

- China produces more steel than Brazil, Russia, Ukraine, Germany, India, South Korea, and the United States combined.

- Iron is the world's most commonly used metal, with 98 percent of all iron ore earmarked for steelmaking.

- Coal is the fastest growing fossil fuel of the last century. The Asia Pacific region accounts for 90 percent of its demand growth.

- If shipping rates are on the rise, investors should increase their exposure to bulk commodities such as coal, iron ore, and steel, which are all moved internationally by sea.

- To keep tabs on global shipping rates, the Baltic Dry Index (BDI) is your best guide.

- Unlike most other commodities, iron ore and coal don't have a futures contract for investors to trade.

- Investors looking to bulk up their portfolios should consider investing in the companies that produce iron ore, coal, and steel.

Chapter Eleven

Capitalizing on Commodities

Why Commodities Are Happening

OPENING YOUR MIND TO THE WORLD OF COMMODITIES is much more than a great investment idea—it's crucial to your overall success as an investor. Once you realize that commodities are *real* things—the rubber that meets the road in any economic expansion—you'll also realize the broad investment implications of rising commodity prices. Currencies, real estate, inflation, stocks, and bonds are all impacted when commodities are on fire.

When demand for commodities is strong, countries rich in natural resources are great places to look for solid investment opportunities, and not just in commodities, but in real estate, currencies, and the stocks of the commodity-producing companies too. A solid understanding of commodities will give you insight into the way the world works and into why some investments soar while others slump. Knowing something about commodities means that everyday activities like shopping for groceries or paying at the pump are no longer simply chores—they become important windows on the world. Adding commodities to your investment portfolio is an investment move that isn't just timely—it's savvy.

Armed with an understanding of commodities, you'll realize the way the world works and why some investments will soar while others will slump.

Maxed Out

The collective credit cards of the Western world are maxed out. More than 20 years of consuming too much and saving too little has finally come home to roost in the most dramatic way. The global financial crisis of 2008–2009 swept back the curtain on the world economy and exposed the rot within. The bursting of the bubble led to the first worldwide recession since the 1930s and left a massive burden of debt now weighing on most of the West.

As the world economy hung in the balance, some of the world's biggest banks went bust while others circled the drain. *"Bailout!"* became the rallying cry of the day as governments were forced to perform emergency triage on their badly ailing financial systems. And in the aftermath of the banking bust-up, rumblings of the next economic crisis can already be heard.

As tax revenues tumble and government expenditures skyrocket, there is reason to worry that the banking crisis has simply morphed into a long-term government debt crisis; a situation that's likely to get worse as the cost of retirees' benefits gets set to explode. These difficulties aren't limited to North America; the markets recently shifted their focus from the eye-popping deficits in Washington and concentrated instead on the fiscal follies in Europe. The most problem-plagued borrowers have been given a disparaging nickname by traders—PIIGS—an acronym for Portugal, Italy, Ireland, Greece, and Spain. The financial markets are obsessed with the PIIGS, and global investors have little confidence that these countries will be able to repay the crushing government debts they face.

Belt Tightening

Governments forced to the wall by their addiction to debt are nothing new. But with no shortage of troubled assets to be mopped up by governments around the world, investors are right to worry about where the money will come from to pay for the mess made by too much government spending. The money may simply be created. After all, America managed to monetize away its debts after both the Second World War and the Vietnam War by printing additional money when its debt load got too high. And without fail, whenever and wherever the printing presses have been turned on to monetize away a country's debts, a bout of inflation has always followed.

The cycle of greed and fear and its economic consequences are all part of the indelible landscape of investing. In 2001, Argentina found itself mired in a sea of debt. Its solution was to default on its sovereign obligations. The repercussions of Argentina's actions came swiftly— there was a sharp currency devaluation, a deep recession, and Argentina became a pariah nation in the international capital markets.

In January 2010, the McKinsey Global Institute conducted a study on the economic consequences of debt and deleveraging. In the study, the authors examined 45 historical episodes of deleveraging where governmental, business, and household debts were shed since 1930. The study found that there were four paths that a highly leveraged economy could take to get rid of its debts. It could: enter a prolonged period of austerity, default on the debts, inflate away the debts, or experience a period of rapid growth where it is able to outgrow its debt burden.

The authors of the McKinsey study found that the austerity, or belt tightening, response was by far the most common approach—occurring in roughly half of the historical examples. These were painful episodes that often lasted for more than six years. The authors concluded that many of the largest economies in the world should expect years of debt reduction in specific sectors of their economies, which will act as a significant drag on GDP growth. The other significant conclusion the researchers came to was that a country's ability to respond to a financial crisis is related to its debt burden prior to the crisis.

Deleveraging after a financial crisis is a painful process and is often a significant drag on GDP.

Asian Ascension

Not surprisingly, the countries with the most robust economies today are the ones that went into the global financial crisis with their economic houses in order: the emerging market economies. With large foreign currency reserves, a growing middle class, and a cultural propensity to work hard and save, the future will belong to Asia. Unfortunately for the West, the trend toward higher, not lower, levels of government debt seems assured. Recent research from the International Monetary Fund (IMF) forecasts that the developing economies should show stable debt trends through 2014, while the developed economies of the West are expected to see escalating government debt.

The underlying trend is undeniable. Asia, led by China, is on an upward economic trajectory. Between 2000 and 2008, 60 percent of the increase in global economic output occurred in the developing world—a trend expected to continue. After decades of gorging on consumption, Americans have turned thrifty while Asians are spending more.

Demand for cars in China is so high that would-be drivers are putting their names on waiting lists for popular models. Also in 2009, China overtook the U.S. for the first time as the largest single market for cars. But it's not just cars for which China is becoming *the* dominant consumer market—it's also the world's biggest market for appliances and desktop computers. In 2009, for example, 185 million refrigerators were sold in China compared with 137 million sold in the American market.

As Chinese and Indian consumers cross the income threshold at which cars and other big-ticket items become affordable, they will become the spark to ignite the commodity price rally. Cars, homes, and appliances are *the* big influences on the global demand for commodities. But best yet, China has ample room to consume more. Not only are the government's coffers full of cash, but the savings rate is close to 40 percent, suggesting that Chinese consumers have the potential to buy even more in the future.

$\sim$

As Chinese and Indian consumers cross the income thresholds at which cars and other big-ticket items become affordable, they will be the spark to ignite the commodity price rally.

Buy Low, Sell High

During the summer of 2009, ships waiting to unload at China's booming Qingdao Port were lined up 10 deep. Piled high with iron ore, coal, crude oil, and other raw materials, up to 90 ships at a time reportedly waited for up to two weeks to unload their precious cargoes. According to J.P. Morgan, Chinese coal imports were 168 percent higher in April of 2009 than they were a year earlier, refined copper imports jumped 148 percent, and iron ore imports were up 33 percent. With an almost insatiable appetite for commodities, China has used the financial crisis to its advantage by stockpiling these basic raw materials of industrialization. Not only is China the largest market for most commodities, it's also one of the savviest buyers of them.

Beijing's interest in commodities is more than good trade—it's good strategy. In an attempt to build a strategic cache of oil and other crucial raw materials in case of a crisis in the Middle East or other key supply region, China has been stockpiling commodities for years. The other key reason the government is actively growing its commodity stockpiles is as a hedge away from risky U.S. dollar investments and toward hard assets whose value can't be inflated away.

Chinese Premier Wen Jiabao has openly stated his concern about the safety of U.S. Treasuries and called on the U.S. "to guarantee the safety of China's assets." With a hoard of more than $750 billion in U.S. Treasuries, China is justifiably worried that the hundreds of billions of dollars the U.S. has spent on bank bailouts will result in a weaker dollar and higher inflation. Amid these concerns, China's stockpiling of commodities gives it a way to reallocate its sovereign wealth. It's even been rumored that China is looking to buy Canadian dollars in an attempt to shield the world's largest currency reserves from a decline in the greenback.

As China's economic influence has increased, the Chinese Investment Corp. (CIC) has emerged as one of the world's largest and most important investors. The hulking $200 billion sovereign wealth fund has been buying up stakes in global resource companies. The CIC has a $652 million stake in Brazilian iron ore giant Vale SA, has invested $1.5 billion in Teck Resources Ltd., and also owns stakes in both ArcelorMittal and Freeport McMoRan Copper and Gold Inc.

The sharp drop in commodity prices in 2008 created an ideal opportunity for investors to jump into the fray. During 2009, the S&P GSCI Index of 24 commodities rose rapidly as lead and sugar doubled in price and gold hit new highs—a move that's beginning to get a lot of attention. According to Barclays Capital, commodities attracted a record $60 billion in 2009, as investors sought to diversify their assets away from more traditional investments.

Bonanza

The global economic playing field has tilted irrevocably toward Asia. What the global financial collapse of 2008–2009 made plain was a trend more than 30 years in the making: Asia is rising. And that's a good news story for commodities, the critical feedstock of urbanization and industrialization.

The West, on the other hand, faces years of slower-than-average economic growth and painful deleveraging. The decade from 2000 to 2009 was notable for negative equity returns in many major stock markets as well as rising levels of unemployment. Facing these headwinds, the future for most of the developed West looks sluggish at best. Yet the prospects for Asia have never looked better. The continent with the money and the people is about to take center stage once again. And as Asia continues its inevitable ascent, hundreds of millions of new global consumers will be created and a bonanza for commodities is likely to ensue.

Many investors have reached a fork in the investment road. They can continue down the one they've always traveled—their portfolios stuffed full of stocks, bonds, and real estate. But from 2000 to 2009, that road led nowhere. Alternatively, investors can choose the road that isn't particularly well traveled but that's been proven to chop risk and boost returns by including commodities in an investment portfolio. This road directly links the West with the East—the epicenter of future economic growth. Investors face a choice: they can invest as they always have, with similar results, or they can buy commodities whose fortunes are tied to the surging economies of Asia.

Hot Commodities

- Knowing something about commodities isn't just timely, it's savvy.

- The authors of the McKinsey Global Institute study concluded that deleveraging after a financial crisis was a painful process that often acted as a significant drag on GDP.

- The underlying trend is undeniable: Asia, led by China, is on an upward economic trajectory.

- As Chinese and Indian consumers cross the income thresholds at which cars and other big-ticket items become affordable, they will be the spark to ignite the commodity price rally.